The Abundant Bohemian

The Abundant Bohemian

Joseph Downing

Boyle
&
Dalton

Book Design & Production
Columbus Publishing Lab
www.ColumbusPublishingLab.com

Print ISBN 978-1-63337-013-5
E-book ISBN 978-1-63337-014-2

Printed in the United States of America
1 3 5 7 9 10 8 6 4 2

Dedicated to the memory of Linda Downing

Table of Contents

"What is it, Ben?" said Mr. Braddock.

"I'm just..." Ben started.

"Worried?"

"Well..."

"About what?"

"I guess about my future."

"What about it?"

"I don't know...I want it to be..."

"To be what?"

"To be different."

From: *The Graduate*

Ernest Hemingway with Lady Duff Twysden, Hadley Hemingway, and three
unidentified people at a café in Pamplona, Spain, during the Fiesta of San
Fermin in July, 1925. Photograph in the Ernest Hemingway Collection, John
F. Kennedy Presidential Library and Museum, Boston.

Part I

The Unconventional Life

The Bud Loosens

*And the day came when the risk to remain tight in a bud was more
painful than the risk it took to blossom.*

Anaïs Nin

Let me set the stage: five attorneys in a conference room sitting
around a long, glass-topped table. The style of the table walks the thin line
between tasteful and ostentatious, as does the framed prints of English fox
hunting scenes that hang on one wall. Bookshelves line the opposite wall,
stacked with dusty legal volumes that are kept more for decoration than
practical use. Opposite the door is a broad window, allowing the dull sun of
early spring to highlight dust particles drifting through the air.

Although women have practiced with the firm in the past, none do
currently, and the five conservatively-suited men each sit with a series of
reports spread before them: hours worked, hours billed, billed hours collected, billed hours outstanding. Each of the attorneys has achieved the status of partner; associate attorneys and staff are not included in the meeting.
The managing partner speaks on what needs to be done to increase revenue
(more hours worked) and complains about the fees that have gone uncol-
lected. It is a talk the attorneys have heard each month for years running.
He reaches for the report on hours billed and outstanding more than sixty
days, but can't find it. While he is looking through his stack, the conversation among the five shifts to other concerns.

"I'm sick of Nick coming in after seven-thirty. It's bullshit."

"Yeah, but he stays late. He puts in more hours than anybody."

"He should be the first one here and the last to leave. A partner shouldn't
have to make the coffee. I'm sick of making the Goddamn coffee."

"Sarah's been walking around in her bare feet again. Now *that's* bullshit. I've already told her not to once. It's...unhygienic."

"Forget Sarah. Did you see that Smith & Smith hired another associate? Where are they getting the work?"

"Nick has only joined the Rotary Club and the Festival Committee. He knows he's required to volunteer at a minimum of three community services groups. If he doesn't join another by the end of the month, I vote to fire him."

"That's a bit over the top."

"Not when you factor in the Goddamn coffee."

"Where's Megan with the sixty-day-bills-outstanding reports?" the manager asks.

"She said she gave them to Joe."

"Joe, do you have them?"

"Joe?"

Outside the window, on the other side of the parking lot, stands a line of evergreen trees, each planted uniformly to separate the residential area from the commercial complex. Beneath one tree a squirrel scurries around, burying bits of food for a future day of need. On a limb on that same tree serenely sits a yellow canary.[1] One attorney, Joe, stares through the window at these two creatures. He knows the canaries pass through this part of the country on their migration north, but it is rare to see one. He is transfixed. After a moment the canary takes flight, disappears from the frame of the window, and Joe experiences an irrational sense of loss. And envy. The squirrel continues his digging.

"Joe!"

Joe turns from the window to the voice.

"Care to join us?" the Partner says, mock-affably, with unhidden irritation.

Joe looks at the four other attorneys, men he has worked with, and generally liked, for seven years.

"I have to go," he says.

---

1 This bird turned out to be an American goldfinch, not a canary, but I didn't know that at the time.

৩৩

To state the obvious, Joe is me. And although the dialogue is a composite of many meetings (lost in my daydream, I hadn't paid any attention to what was being said that particular day), it represents the same meeting I attended once a month for seven years. I did see the squirrel and the canary that day, and the obvious and not-so-unique metaphor that they represented helped me pull the trigger, but I knew for some time I was allowing my soul to die a slow death. And I knew I couldn't do it any more. But knowing that and knowing what to *do* about it are two very different things. What next? And *how?* That can be a very scary question, and a difficult one to answer.

৩৩

I was a good kid; I did what I was told. I listened to my parents and my teachers. I got good grades. I went to college. I worked hard as a student and worked hard at a factory boxing brake linings in the summer to make money for school. And when I graduated, I got a good job wearing a suit and tie at the city power company. *A good job*—the holy grail of success in America had been reached. I had done what I was supposed to do.

But I was miserable. Company policy permitted men to wear only white or blue dress shirts and no facial hair was allowed. Employees had to park facing *in*—your car could not be facing *out*. Only two personal items were allowed per cubicle. I worked for a year before I was fired due to my bad attitude and lack of team spirit. I suffered from a deep depression; I couldn't understand what was wrong with me, why I had such a hard time fitting in with the real world. My confidence and self-esteem hit an all-time low, and I didn't know what to do next. I thought long and hard and did what any driven, middle class college graduate with a liberal arts degree would do: I went to law school.

After graduating, I took a job with the previously-described law firm. But my work life wasn't much different than it was with the power company. In addition to the pointless meetings, the managing partner told the rest of us where to live, where to eat, what clubs to join. I was making decent money, but no more than many of my friends with less education and seemingly a lot less job stress. My depression returned. Toward the end of my seven years with my firm, a partner in a large, prestigious law firm approached me and offered a job. Not just any job, but *the* job, the coveted job that everyone wanted in law school, the kind for which only the top 10% of students were even granted an interview. This job was the Powerball of the legal market. The results of getting this opportunity led to the canary day and the regaining of my life.

I met the partner, Jim, for dinner one Friday night at 6:00 p.m. in early summer at a plush, old-school steakhouse in the city. The evening was sunny and warm, but it could have been any season in the window-less, dark-wooded, leather-boothed dining room. The patrons were mostly middle-aged business types, still in their suits. Martinis, wine and red meat topped most tables. Jim arrived late, his eyes baggy, his tie loose. He smiled and shook my hand with the expected firmness. He was cordial, polished, complimentary. I was impressed and a little intimidated. We discussed the type of work I would be doing, and I asked questions about the firm and his practice. He liked me. I liked him. He offered me the job, with a salary doubling what I was currently making. I couldn't help but be pleased and excited. When people say you've made it, this is what they mean.

Joseph Downing

⟲◎

My father was an artist, although he would deny it if asked. He would call himself a *commercial* artist, or, specifically (like his hero, N. C. Wyeth, in his later years when clouded in self-doubt) an illustrator. Growing up, I didn't care—all I knew was my dad could *draw*, and that made his job much cooler than the jobs my friends' fathers had, whatever it was they did with their briefcases and ties. By the time I was eight, he turned freelance and worked from home where he was around all day to inspire and encourage the creativity of my younger brother and me. He bought us drawing boards—the exact replica of his, only child-sized—and gave us unlimited access to his art supplies. While he worked, Scott and I drew and mimicked every move of our father's, staying up past our bedtimes drawing and listening with him to The Stones, The Beatles and Creedence long into the night. He was supportive but could be critical; I wasn't yet able to acknowledge weaknesses and I craved constant praise. Nonetheless, it was bliss. I wrote and illustrated comic books. I painted, I drew. I wrote poetry. There was no past or future. I was just alive and happy.

By the time I turned twelve, computer graphics began taking over the advertising and design world. My father was an ink and paper man; he couldn't, or wouldn't, make the transition. All his industry contacts were retiring or moving on. His contract stream dried up. My mother's career prospered, and she became the breadwinner as my father shifted to househusband and soccer coach. He did the job well, but his self-esteem, I understand now, suffered a substantial blow.

And it was art's fault.

Even in my most rebellious moments, my father's word carried the weight of stone tablets brought down from the mountain. And as his bitterness against art and the business of art grew, so did mine. So when he told me to stay away from it, I took him very literally. Despite spending some of the happiest moments of my life with a marker or a paintbrush in my hand, at age fourteen I quit drawing completely. I don't remember it being a hard or heavy decision at the time. I had started high school, and playing soccer, dating girls, and dealing with the many other challenges and opportunities that hit us as early adolescents were enough to occupy me. I felt no loss, no sense of grief. That was to come much later.

When I applied to college all I knew was that I didn't want to be poor any more. Despite having no interest or aptitude for either science or math, my major was pre-med for no other reason than the belief that doctors were respected and made a lot of money. That lasted a year. Reality kicked in when my grades came out and I drifted, undeclared, until my junior year. In my American literature class, a professor and future mentor praised a paper I had written on *The Scarlet Letter*, and his praise meant much more to me than it should have. The praise was deserved, but it showed I was starved for something that I didn't understand I needed. I could read and I could write—that much I knew. English became my major, I graduated, I got a job.

After the failed year at the power company I faced the dilemma that all liberal arts majors face—what the hell do you do with the degree? I took all the tests: the GMAT, the GRE, the LSAT. I did very well on the LSAT, so well that I applied to law school and received a substantial scholarship offer. I was also offered a grad assistantship to pursue a Master's in English, with the idea of teaching someday. I asked my father what he thought I should do. I'm sure my question stirred up memories of the months that went by between the contracts he received and the feast or famine lifestyle that came with working in the arts. I certainly remembered them.

"Go to law school, for Christ sakes. Make some money."

And I did.

My interview with Jim wound down and we moved to idle chitchat about families and hobbies. As he was paying the check, almost as an afterthought, I asked him why he wanted to hire me.

"It took years of hard work to make partner and I'm finally feeling comfortable enough that I can share the workload with someone else. Now

I want to slow down and spend more time with my daughter before she leaves for college."

I could respect that. I asked him how old she was.

"She's seventeen. She's going to Penn State in the fall." He pulled out his wallet and showed me a photo of a young woman in a volleyball uniform, smiling for the camera. His daughter who was leaving for college in less than six months.

We talked a bit longer and then he said he needed to get back to the office to wrap up a few things before he went home. It was 7:30 on a Friday night. His secretary would email the job details on Monday. We shook hands and I left to meet friends and he headed back to his desk. At my car I stopped and watched him walk across the parking lot. He was my height, my build, and from the back, it was easy to envision I was looking at my future self.

I sat in the driver's seat a long time before starting the engine. I was no longer excited or proud; I was scared and depressed. *I can't do this*, I thought. Something inside me had shifted. He was offering me the Golden Fleece and after seeing it up close, I didn't want it. I didn't want to be that prematurely aged man, heading back to his office, looking for a way to squeeze a last bit of joy from the sliver remaining of his daughter's youth. Still, I doubted myself, thinking about the money and security it would bring and the stuff I could buy. I questioned my motives. Was I scared, afraid I couldn't handle it, didn't have what it takes? Was I just lazy? But I couldn't escape the image of him walking back to his office on a Friday night, the office where a picture of his daughter from ten years ago, young, pig-tailed and wishing her father was home, surely sat on his desk. On Monday morning I declined the offer.

What is important about this story is not its uniqueness, but its commonality. It's a story so many of us share. We are told to be safe, cautious and realistic by our parents, teachers and community. We are told to work hard now—there will be time for other things later. These people mean well. It's their job to guide us and protect us from harm. They want us to have a steady income and insurance to cover every potential disaster. Few things are more painful to parents than to see their child suffer or fail. They advise us to trade passion for security and we, dutiful children that we are, listen, and give up being painters or marine biologists to be lawyers, accountants, engineers and insurance salesmen and live lives pushing the "what if" thoughts away with new toys and antidepressants.

Because who wants the other option? It's true that some musicians, actors and artists break through and become rich and successful, but they are the exception, not the rule. Most scratch out a meager existence waiting tables and washing dishes to pay the rent in their 6 x 8 studio apartment in Greenwich Village.

I'm not bashing traditional careers like lawyer, accountant, or insurance salesman. After all, I'm one of them. I'm saying that to give up what feeds our souls for reasons of security, creature comforts or societal pressure is choosing a slow death. The good news is that we don't have to make a choice: we can have both. We can ease our parents' and our own fears by having a job with a steady income and still be fully engaged in the lives we want, pursuing our passions and living by our own rules. People have accomplished this throughout the millennia and we can too.

The interview with Jim that fateful night shook my moorings, and I was depressed and directionless for some time. I began writing fiction, and slowly recovered what it felt like to be passionate about something. I put a plan into action. I put money away and a year later (Canary Day) I quit the firm and opened my own law practice. My office was smaller and less grandiose, but was tasteful and sufficient. I split space with another attorney and hired a secretary to work only part time, reducing my overhead by 80%. All of my clients followed me to my new office. My first year on my own I made more money than my best year with the firm; the following year I did even better, improving each subsequent year. Since I no longer had partners to answer to, reports to review or office squabbles to resolve, I worked fewer hours and with this extra time I wrote and pursued things that inspire me.

Making the decision to leave a comfortable but unsatisfying job was not easy. I convinced myself that I was going to fail. I was going to go bankrupt. I was going to starve. I wasn't good enough and I didn't know what I was doing. I had started thinking of other part-time jobs I would need to work in order to pay my bills while my law practice floundered. But none of these self-defeating fantasies came true and the extremity of my fears seems ridiculous in hindsight. But they didn't then. I very easily could have changed my mind, and I almost did many times.

If this story sounds familiar, it's time to take stock and decide how long you are willing to set aside the life you really want to live. This book will help you get there, but don't expect any magic revelations. I don't have a secret five step plan to achieve complete fulfillment. Some of what I write about I've achieved and some remains aspirational. The purpose of this book is to give you courage, support, and the strength to do what you need to do, so that when you're ninety you aren't sitting by the window reflecting upon your life and crying into your fiber supplement. If you feel this way, you already are a Bohemian at heart whether you describe yourself as one or not. But soon enough, I believe that you will know you are one, like I do now, and you'll find a whole new road open before you on our shared journey.

The Abundant Bohemian

*I'm a girl from a good family who was very well brought up. One day I
turned my back on it all and became a Bohemian.*

Brigitte Bardot

What is a Bohemian?

It's very simple. Webster's Dictionary defines a Bohemian as: a person living an unconventional life.

That's it. *To live an unconventional life.* In today's materialistic and frantic culture, the possibility of having an unconventional life is so appealing, and yet for most, seemingly unattainable. We have too many responsibilities, too many obligations, too many bills to pay. Who has time to take the afternoon off and paint in the park? But it is possible to live an unconventional life and pay your bills at the same time.

It may be difficult at first to simplify our understanding of a Bohemian, because most of us think of the term as describing some variation of a beret-wearing, money-starved, suffering artist discussing avant-garde performance art or eastern European film in a coffee shop. In 1851 this definition became the norm when Henri Murger wrote *Scènes de la Vie de Bohème*, the story of his life as an impoverished writer living in an attic in Paris's Left Bank. His novel was made into a play, the play was the inspiration for Puccini's Opera, *La Bohème*, and the definition was firmly planted into modern culture. In *Status Anxiety,*[i] the philosopher and writer Alain de Botton takes the description a bit further:

They dressed simply; they lived in the cheaper parts of town; they read a lot; they seemed not to care much about money; they were frequently of melancholic temperament; their allegiances were to art and emotion rather than to business and material success; they sometimes had unconven-

11

tional sexual lives and some of the women wore their hair short before it was the fashion.

This mirrors what Bertram Wolfe, biographer of artist Diego Rivera, saw among the Bohemians in Diego's Parisian crowd in the early 20th century. He found that they treated dress, drink, sex and money lightly, but were dead serious about art. "Indeed in [art and ideas about art] all truth, honor, beauty and devotion lodged, for they were the *raison d'être* of Bohemia."

I found that many people respond emotionally to the word "Bohemian." Conservatives tended to equate it with being leftist and anti-establishment. And many creative folk were snobbishly dismissive, believing that Bohemia had become a cliché. For the hipsters, if the bourgeoisie even *knew* about the term Bohemian, it was too mainstream for them.

In 1961 psychiatrist Francis J. Rigney and psychologist L. Douglas Smith decided to solve the Bohemian question once and for all and conducted a year-long research project, "using the techniques of psychiatry and psychology to evaluate, both scientifically and personally, the nature [of the Bohemian]"*, which they documented in their book, *The Real Bohemia*.[ii] The results were mixed at best and are now entertainingly comic in their datedness. (At the beginning of the book they provide a "definitions" section, so that the reader can understand the lingo of the Bohemian. An example: "cornball" means "a square, who is also a yokel." They are careful to define the Bohemian's use of the words 'man' and 'like.' They write, "man is used as a kind of *formal address,* similar to the honorifics of German and other languages, e.g., *mein Herr.* [Like] is used to *call attention to,* or emphasize, that which follows; for example, 'Like, what are you doing, man?'") A common response by the Bohemians to their questionnaire: "How in God's name are these stupid questions going to show anything about anything?" Their scientific method wasn't very enlightening.

So there it is in a nutshell: floating somewhere between a beatnik and a hippie, an artist and an outcast; someone who has stepped out of the mainstream and flouts conventional morals and values; someone who praises art but despises money, and in contemporary times, mistrusted by both the left and the right. And like many stereotypes, it is both right and wrong. Being a Bohemian can be so much less, and so much more. Being Bohemian *may* include these attributes, but they are not essential. You don't have to choose between starving artist or spoiled bourgeoisie. Botton writes, "Bohemians could be found in every social class, age group, and profession: they were men and women, rich and poor, poets and lawyers, scientists and the unemployed." And Botton quotes Arthur Ransome saying as early as 1907 that Bohemia can be anywhere because it is not a place but a state of mind.

And what is an unconventional life? Webster's helps us with that one also: *not bound by or in accordance with convention; being out of the ordinary.* And that year-long psychological study performed by Rigney and Smith? The primary, and certainly one of the few, conclusions that they drew from their scientific study of Bohemians was that "the majority saw themselves, above all, as nonconformists." You can be a scientist, doctor, lawyer, or candlestick maker and have a life out of the ordinary, a life not defined by others' rules. That is living a Bohemian life.[2] And for so many of us, the time for that has come.

Why now?

The fact to which we have got to cling, as to a lifebelt, is that it is possible to be a normal decent person and yet be fully alive.
Allen Ginsberg

Therein lies the problem: so many of us have followed the rules and achieved the success society told us we wanted, and yet something crucial is missing. What's missing is the feeling of being *fully alive*. If being unconventional means being out of the ordinary, I would expand it to mean being *extra*ordinary; to be the kind of person Jack Kerouac praises:

---

2 I originally wanted to call this book *The Bourgeois Bohemian* until I discovered author David Brooks had already coined this phrase to describe the "new upper middle class" that "believes that spending $15,000 on a media center is vulgar, but that spending $15,000 on a slate shower stall is a sign that you are at one with the Zenlike rhythms of nature." This book is not about those people.

Here's to the crazy ones, the misfits, the rebels, the troublemakers, the round pegs in the square holes...the ones who see things differently – they're not fond of rules... You can quote them, disagree with them, glorify or vilify them, but the only thing you can't do is ignore them because they change things...they push the human race forward, and while some may see them as the crazy ones, we see genius, because the ones who are crazy enough to think that they can change the world, are the ones who do.[iii]

We all have the capacity, the talent, the inner sacred *humanness* to live extraordinary lives. But it takes courage. Courage, imagination and resilience, spiced with a touch of rebellion. We're all dreamers, and some dream more than others. Ignore those dreams at your own peril. Follow those dreams and the stodgy and security-obsessed won't make it easy on you. Rule followers don't like rule breakers. But others with grand imaginations who refuse to settle for the status quo exist, too. Being who you really are will draw these people into your life. Salman Rushdie, in *The Ground Beneath Her Feet*, says it beautifully:

In every generation there are a few souls, call them lucky or call them cursed, who are simply born not belonging . . . there may even be millions, billions of such souls, as many non-belongers as belongers, perhaps . . . [But] those who value stability, who fear transience, uncertainty, change, have erected a powerful system of stigmas and taboos against rootlessness, that disruptive, anti-social force, so that we mostly conform, we pretend to be motivated by loyalties and solidarities we do not really feel, we hide our secret identities beneath the false skins of those identities which bear the belongers' seal of approval. But the truth leaks out in our dreams.[iv]

We all need support and guidance along our journey and for this we can draw from mentors, trailblazers, and shamans. Henry Miller, Tom Robbins, Lin Yutang, and the fictional character Zorba the Greek from the novel of the same name are a few of mine. We can find inspiration from the stories and wisdom from great Bohemian thinkers throughout the ages and the not-so-famous Bohemians living extraordinary lives quietly and probably next door to you. I ask that you join me in asking the tough questions required to move toward the authentic lives we all crave. When you need a push to get going or to quell the doubts that will inevitably creep back in, their stories will remind you that you are not alone. As Buddhist teacher Thich Nhat Hanh wrote, "the truth is already inside you. A teacher can only offer you the chance to awaken your true self." We need to draw from the resources that remind us that yes, we are living the life meant for us and we are not crazy, no matter what the Chamber of Commerce or the PTA think about it.

It's time to conquer that fear and start living the unconventional life you've always wanted. Anaïs Nin reached a point in life where the impetus to grow and live more intensely became so powerful that she could no longer resist it. I reached that place in my own life and you probably have as well. It's time to be Bohemian.

Reigniting Your Passion

Payne seized her. They grappled lovingly among the hampers. A famous man says that we go through life with "a diminishing portfolio of enthusiasms"; and these, these, these children, these these these these little children will soon not be able to feel this way about anything again.

Thomas McGuane, from *The Bushwhacked Piano*

A diminishing portfolio of enthusiasms. I think we all know what he means. But why does it have to be so? Why do we give up our enthusiasms so easily and without a fight? Does it happen so slowly that we don't notice until they're gone? I was once asked what I missed most about being five years old. My answer was that I missed instantaneous access to unfettered joy. Watch a child in a park spinning in circles and giggling until she falls down dizzy and you'll know what I mean. Watch an adult do the same thing, and see how long it takes for the cops to show up. Why is it so hard to dance without inhibition once we become adults? Some of us still can. But many of us need intoxicants to attack our brain inhibitors before we can let loose.

Look at your own portfolio of enthusiasms. How's it holding up? I bet it's lighter than it was when you were five, fifteen, or twenty years old. Do you play with paint on the picnic table like you did when you were a child? Do you listen to records all the way through—not while doing something else—solely for the pleasure the music gives you, like you did when a teen? Do you make love to your partner with the love, lust, and abandon like you did in your twenties? You probably don't. It's natural to mellow with age. First times only happen once, and newness inevitably wanes. That's okay. Jungian theory has a name for this: growing down. But to give up on our dreams is unacceptable. Aging is no excuse for a passionless,

16

joyless life. And I'm talking big joy, Bohemian joy.

One of the gifts of living the unconventional life is that when you allow yourself to do what you want and what is best for you, everything you experience is more joyful. The flowers are more pungent, work flows easier, music sounds better. Don't mistake this newfound freedom as an excuse to avoid your responsibilities, but as a means to avoid unwanted responsibilities before you incur them. If you want to begin practicing the art of living life to the fullest, taking pure joy in what you have, where you live, and who you live with, you need look no further than the great fictional character created by Nikos Kazantzakis, the man called Zorba the Greek.ᵛ

Zorba the Greek is the story of Basil, a disenchanted Greek intellectual who escapes to the Island of Crete to run a mining company in the 1930s. In doing so he hopes to connect with the peasant folk living on the island whom he believes can show him how to live a more authentic life. He gets this and more when he hires Zorba to help him run the mine. Zorba's lusty zest for life and spiritual guidance pulls Basil out of his shell and awakens him to what it means to fully embrace the joys and sorrows of a life well lived.

Zorba was a Bohemian without knowing it. Nor would he care if someone told him. "Who has time for labels?" he would ask. Zorba was too busy living to waste time worrying about such trivialities. Does making the life changes you want sound too scary? Too risky? That was how Basil felt. When Basil fretted over a petty decision, Zorba said, "What are you thinking about? You keep a pair of scales, too, do you? You weigh everything to the nearest gram, don't you? Come on, friend, make up your mind. Take the plunge!" We lose so many opportunities and waste so much energy weighing everything to the nearest gram, afraid of making the wrong decision. And sometimes we *will* make the wrong decision, there's no way around that, and no amount of fretting will prevent it. Think things through and then be bold. Zorba wasn't afraid to risk failing, and he failed often. But failing means less when you are able to shrug and move on. Zorba was capable of taking knocks and getting up, and that takes courage. Here he is berating Basil again for his hesitancy: "What do you lack? You're young, you have money, health, you're a good fellow, you lack nothing. Nothing, by thunder! Except just one thing—folly! And when that's missing, boss, well . . ." When that's missing, joy is missing. When that is missing we *miss out.* Henry Miller agrees. "Why are we so full of restraint?" he wrote. "Why do we not give in all directions? Is it fear of losing ourselves? Until we do lose ourselves there is no hope of finding ourselves."

The sad fact is, we do lose ourselves, but not in the freeing way Miller describes. Like rust, complacency, lack of focus, and escapism creep into our lives subtly and we don't notice this until one day, years later, we wake up and don't recognize our own lives. This awakening tends to come from a radical life change, such as a health scare, divorce, job loss, or death of a loved one. But we don't have to—and we simply *can't*—wait for that to happen. Make *not waiting* your radical event. And the first radical act is to look honestly, with a scalpel, and see what is holding you back, what illusions and excuses you have made to justify, probably unconsciously, a life of diminishing enthusiasms. Hermann Hesse said, "often I tried the frightening way of 'reality,' where things that count are profession, law, fashion, finance. But disillusioned and freed I fled away alone to the other side, the place of dreams and blessed folly." *Folly.* Zorba, like Hess, knew folly's value. Folly is defined as acting without good sense or normal prudence, and the sensible and prudent will be happy to point out your bad decisions if you "fail." But they are also happy to follow your newly blazed trail when you defy their expectations and make a new, more interesting path on which to journey.

Much of the blame for our loss of enthusiasms can be placed on the way we choose to earn money. We place too much value on security and give up too many of our freedoms out of fear, need, and a desire for stuff. We allow work to sap us of our energy, our passions and our time. We are too damn tired to live. Oh, the hours, the days, the years I've wasted in the mundane, the unimportant, on agendas not my own! But it doesn't have to be that way. We can bring passion and creativity to whatever we do. The idea that "you're not supposed to like it—that's why it's called work," is destructive and unnecessary. We need to assess what "work" can do for us and what we can do with it. We need to challenge the way we view money, how we get it, and how we spend it. To live unconventionally, you will need to look at all the rules you've subjected yourself to and put them all up for reconsideration. The time to do this is now.

Part II

Freedom, Work and Money

The cost of a thing is the amount of what I call life which is required to be exchanged for it, immediately or in the long run.

Henry David Thoreau

Forget Security

Chase after money and security and your heart will never unclench.

The Tao Te Ching

First say to yourself what you would be, and then do what you have to do.

Epictetus

In the summer of 2008 a friend invited me to what she called a Ga-looka Party in my hometown of Dayton. When I asked what that was, she described it as part art show, live concert, performance art exhibition, and general big party. It was held in a warehouse in the city and when we arrived it was packed. Multiple artists' work hung on the walls and wood and steel sculptures were displayed throughout the cavernous room. A band was playing on a stage near the bar and people were drinking, dancing, mingling and carousing. If this were the 1960s, the scene would have been called a "happening." I asked my friend who was responsible for creating the event and she pointed to a thirty-something man in a secondhand white tuxedo with dreadlocks stretching down to his belt. That's how I met Shon Walters.

Watching his exuberance on stage and in group performance pieces, it's hard to reconcile his quiet, thoughtful, even shy, nature when conversing with him directly. Despite routinely having his art selected for prestigious national art exhibitions and festivals, he lives simply in a small house in the city that he has rehabbed from the studs up. He works with wood, sculpting sensual, almost feminine pieces that are remarkable in their intricacy and delicacy. His art resembles no other. He makes a living doing what he loves and creating beautiful things. I know this level of success doesn't happen over night and I wanted to know how he got here.

By the time he was in the ninth grade, he knew that wood sculpture was his calling. Having this self-knowledge, after high school he moved from Dayton to rural Athens, Ohio to live in an old farmhouse with several roommates. Why Athens? One, it was inexpensive, and his minimal living costs provided the time he needed to hone his craft. But more importantly, his farmhouse was attached to eighty acres of forest, a woodworker's paradise.

In preparing to move he worked in a Dayton factory that, provided the employee worked a full twelve-hour shift, allowed a flexible schedule. He could show up for two days, take days off and then go back; he could work fifty days in a row if he liked. Working twenty days straight provided enough money to live in Athens for a *year*, thereby freeing up time to work on his art. One day in the farmhouse Shon told his roommate that his coffee table was ugly and proposed that he make him a new one provided they throw the current one away. His friend agreed. He made a table from wood he found in the forest using only a drill, a drill bit, an X-Acto knife, and a chisel. Everyone liked it, and he began to get commissions from friends and others who liked his work. Momentum began.

Down the road from his home was a commercial building of unknown purpose (the building had no signage or windows) but stacked outside were cut logs Shon thought would be useful for chair making. He stopped by one day when the owner was in the yard and the man agreed to let Shon have some of the wood. After Shon told him of his plans to make chairs, he asked Shon to bring a finished one by. It turned out the man was a cabinet-maker and trained sculptor and the building was his wood shop. When he saw the workmanship of the chair, he offered Shon a job. Momentum grew.

From 5:00 a.m. to 9:00 a.m. Shon worked on his art with the vast array of tools in the shop, worked for the owner until 5:30 p.m., and then went back to his own art in the evening. It took two years of constant work for him to discover his style.

He moved back to Dayton and became a respected, well-known and well-sold artist, both locally and nationally. He teaches woodworking part-

time (fifteen hours a week) but
he is otherwise supported by
his art. He was offered a full-
time teaching job with benefits
at a local high school, but he
wouldn't have time to do his
own work. He has had offers
for well-paying, full-time em-
ployment at cabinet shops, but
would make nothing but boxes
all day. These opportunities
would have provided a secure
paycheck, but they would have
forced him to put his passion—
his true purpose—second.
And that is something he is
unwilling to trade for security.
"I don't think I've ever questioned my path or doubted my
choices," he told me.

Flower Power by Shon Walters. Photograph by Josh Mayes.

Why is Shon's story important? Because he didn't let the need for security derail him from pursuing his passion and calling. Fear's biggest ally
is the illusion of security. People will sacrifice their dreams, their hopes
and their aspirations for the guarantee of a paycheck that will come week
after week and year after year. And this "guarantee" that we value so much,
if it ever was true, is no more. Our economy is in constant flux and the
company job that a worker kept for fifty years is gone. People wake up
every day, work fifty plus hours a week, spend every penny they have on
diversions and junk they don't need to compensate for the lack of inspiration they receive in their daily lives, and then are let go when they can be

replaced by cheap overseas labor or fresh-faced college graduates who will do the same work for half the costs. Most Americans do not have enough savings to get them through the first month of unemployment. Where is the security that is so prized? It doesn't exist, and it's time to let that myth go.

I'm not advocating reckless behavior, or suggesting that it is wrong to plan ahead for a rainy day. Far from it. I'm advocating not sacrificing your true self for the mistaken belief that you can protect yourself from risk and failure. Shon Walters could have made boxes and possibly could have more money in the bank. At what cost? When practicing his art, he describes the experience as, "Whatever the opposite of frustration is; a sense of peacefulness, a heavenly, angelic feeling." Who in the world would trade that experience for more money? Many of us, sadly. One of the wisest things I've read on the subject of risk is from Nadine Stair of Louisville, Kentucky who at eighty-five years old wrote, "If I Had My Life to Live Over":[vi]

I'd like to make more mistakes next time. I'd relax. I would limber up. I would be sillier than I have been this trip. I would take fewer things seriously. I would take more chances. I would climb more mountains and swim more rivers. I would eat more ice cream and less beans. I would perhaps have more actual troubles, but I'd have fewer imaginary ones . . .

If I had my life to live over, I would start barefoot earlier in the spring and stay that way later in the fall. I would go to more dances. I would ride more merry-go-rounds. I would pick more daisies.

Security is an illusion. Make that your mantra. One good friend of mine held on to a corporate job for years despite hating the work because his employer was a Fortune 500 company and he wanted the security that the company provided. He was laid off, of course. When this happened he was depressed and scared but in only a few weeks he got a better job, one that gave him more satisfaction and more pay. His only regret is the years he wasted not making the move on his own.

One attorney I knew expressed his need for security by viewing every person he came in contact with as a potential client, aggressively drumming up business at every turn. His self-serving and insincere manner was evident and many people didn't want to be around the guy.

That attorney's attitude is often shared by people who believe that "life is competition," that someone has to lose in order for someone to win, and that the pie is limited and one needs to grab as much as one can before somebody else gets it. I say we can just make more pies. Sure, competition for customers and clients exists in certain jobs, but "jobs" do not equate to "life," and usually there are plenty of customers to go around for everyone if we're not greedy. Four other attorneys work within one block of my office, and we refer clients back and forth and offer advice and assistance to one another freely. We are busy enough and do just fine. I doubt any of us would be more financially successful if we behaved in a cutthroat "life is competition" manner, but I am sure we would be less happy and more resentful if we did.

The best attitude towards the acceptance of insecurity is that of my friend Arturo, a Mexican immigrant and a restaurateur who left his impoverished rural village and came to the United States when he was sixteen. When he arrived he spoke no English and survived working twelve hours a day bussing tables and washing dishes. Now in his thirties, he owns two successful restaurants and is quite wealthy. Money is a means to an end, and the end is usually a good time with the people he loves. He is generous to a fault, spending freely on his family, friends, and employees. He has given much back to his hometown in Mexico. He shrugs if ever questioned about his free spending. He had nothing once, and he could have nothing again, he says. "If I had to, I could go back to bussing tables. I'll always have a job. I could lose it all someday, and maybe I will. I'm not going to worry about it." This doesn't mean he doesn't get frustrated, stressed, or tired of work. But it does mean he is not afraid. Arturo is happy because he is not attached to his success or the material wealth it brings. He knows he could lose it all, but whatever will be, will be, he believes.

Security is an illusion. The question we must ask ourselves is: how much unhappiness and freedom are we willing to sacrifice in order to maintain this illusion? Another question we must ask is how much *growth* are we willing to give up? Insecurity kicks us into activity; insecurity awakens and enlivens us. Business coach Peter Block agrees: "As long as we wish for safety, we will have difficulty pursuing what matters." We can either risk doing what we want and being who we really want to be, knowing we may fail and suffer for it, or stay in an unsatisfactory position because it is "secure" and suffer and fail anyway. Once one understands that security exists nowhere, it seems insane to restrain oneself. But yet, we still do. It's not easy to step out of our comfort zones. I was in my thirties before I was able to.

The problem with taking risks is that when you don't succeed, it *hurts*. I can't deny that. I have boxfuls of rejection letters for my writing and the cringe I experience when I see that thin envelope in the mail never recedes. My father took a risk when he quit his comfortable job with the advertising agency and went freelance, and there were many times when his freedom made life for my family hard; times when we didn't have groceries in the fridge and didn't know how the mortgage was going to be paid. To make sure you have enough money to buy your child's insulin is a real concern. Let nothing I say make you believe that I am belittling serious needs. But rarely are those the reasons that hold us back. And the hurt that is brother to risk is integral to the process also; it is part of living a full and whole life, not a sheltered half-lived existence. "Ours is a society that conditions us to protect ourselves from any direct difficulty and discomfort," writes Buddhist Jack Kornfield. "We expend enormous energy denying our insecurity, fighting pain, death and loss, and hiding from the basic truths of the natural world and our own nature." The desire for security is the same as the *fear of need*. But this doesn't bear out logically, as Kahlil Gibran recognized when he said, "And what is fear of need but need itself? Is not dread of thirst when your well is full, the thirst that is unquenchable?" I spent my early twenties, years I will never get back, doing work I didn't enjoy (fear of poverty), engaging with people I didn't truly like (fear of loneliness) and *not* doing what I was passionate to do (fear of vulnerability, rejection). I value the lessons those years taught me. But I wish it hadn't taken so long.

If you value security above all else, contentment and fulfillment will be beyond your reach. You'll spend much time looking backward and thinking about all the what-might-have-beens. If you are like me, most of your regrets are for opportunities missed, not opportunities that failed. That girl you wanted to ask out. That business you wanted to start. That book you wanted to write. Woe to those who play it safe and wait. Give up on security.

If jumping off the boat without a life jacket feels too risky for you, then create a safety net. Decide how much money you need to have in reserve for the incubation period for your new business, art project, or adventure. Do you need $5,000 to make your move? $10,000? $30,000? Decide, put a savings plan in place, and follow it. And when you reach your goal, make a commitment to yourself that you will follow through. Just know there will never be a perfect time. If it doesn't work out, it is usually not hard to return to the status quo. An acquaintance working in the human resources division of a large company told me that if an employee leaves his former employer on good terms and gave proper notice, his chances of being rehired are high. The employer already knows the employee's strengths and having that information makes that employee a safer hire than an unknown applicant. The employer also doesn't have to start training from the beginning. Find out your employer's policy, if possible.

Taking risks is not easy; it requires tremendous courage that one must draw upon again and again. We cling to what we know, even if it makes us unhappy, because the unknown is scarier. The courage to give up the illusion of security requires you to accept that nothing is or ever will be certain. It requires you to accept the risks you take every time you step out of your door. It requires you to accept that any choice you make will have consequences, and not always the consequences you had hoped for. But to be alive, to live the unconventional life, that is what we must do. "I am not afraid to make a mistake, even a great mistake, a lifelong mistake, and perhaps as long as eternity, too," James Joyce wrote. Like Joyce, you must also overcome the fear of making a great mistake. If you choose to love deeply, your heart will probably be broken sooner or later. If you choose to express yourself, someone will ridicule or resent you. Any time you choose to do *anything*, you risk failing. You need to feel the fear and move through it, like Joyce did. Be willing to make a great mistake. Give up your search for security—it can't be found. But we can find many beautiful things to take its place.

Work for Yourself

To dance one's life is to understand its rhythms, to become familiar with one's neu-robiological "timepieces," to create the "steps" which suit our personality best, to reawaken the still, small music that plays within us all.

Thierry Paquot

Bohemians, I can't express enough the importance of doing whatever you can to become self-employed. Making the choice to work for oneself is scary—it certainly was for me. But oh how happy I am that I pushed through that fear! Working forty to fifty to sixty hours a week for someone else under their rules—even if you like the work—is toxic; it sucks the joy and life from any vocation. (Be honest: is there *anything* you want to do for eight straight hours five or more days a week, other than sleep?) When I started working for myself I became more productive by working less. This was in part because I shed wasted time lost in pointless and unproductive meetings, employee management, and banal water cooler chitchat. More significantly, I began to work the hours that made sense to me; I worked when I was at the height of my energy and mental effectiveness and then I went home. I no longer wasted time, watching the slow moving clock and waiting for the hand to reach five. Some days I go in early; some days I sleep in. If I'm on a roll I stay late; if I'm tired in the early afternoon I go home. Sometimes I have a quick lunch, other times I have long, languid lunches with friends.

But most importantly, I try to limit the amount of time I spend doing legal work to between four and six hours a day so that I have a couple of hours to express my creative side, which, for me, is writing, with an occasional sprinkling of painting. Rewarding myself with this time is the best compensation I receive from my work. If I worked for a firm, the high billable hour requirements would (and did) leave me so fatigued that I wouldn't have the mental energy to express myself creatively. And that is the trap in which so many of us find ourselves. Our bosses could care less about our true purpose and creative expression. They need us to produce 15% more than we did the previous fiscal year. Our fatigue is not their problem. Get a cup of coffee. Talk to your therapist about your depression. Just make sure the report is on my desk by Monday.

The fundamental problem with the corporate structure as it has evolved in capitalistic systems is that you are either *in*, or you are *out*. You work the fifty plus hours a week or you are replaced by someone who will. One friend, a sales manager for a large company, once told me he did not hire an otherwise qualified applicant for a sales position because that person had taken a year off after graduating college (a common practice in Europe) to work as a ski instructor, his reason being that the applicant clearly lacked drive if he wasted a whole year playing around on the slopes. Another friend, a financial planner, was told by his employer that his five-year-old midmarket sedan didn't evoke the appropriate image of success and that if he wanted to keep his job he needed to upgrade. My friend bought an expensive Audi. You are in, or you are out. And offering time as compensation? It's not in the cards. "With few exceptions, employers (the sellers) don't offer the chance to trade off income gains for a shorter work day or the occasional sabbatical," writes economist Juliet Schor.[vii] "They just pass on income, in the form of annual pay raises or bonuses."

Sigh. It wasn't always this way. In *The Art of the Siesta*,[viii] writer Thierry Paquot discusses how the clock and regimented work structures took over the world, changing the way we worked irrevocably. He writes:

It was probably around 1345 that the division of the hour into sixty minutes, and the minute into sixty seconds, spread throughout the city's ruling classes, transforming each individual's time previously regulated by the rhythms of the heart, of the breath and other activities—into a homogenous, abstract time: the reference point of one time for all . . . But a "watch" only has value so long as mechanical time, machine time—that is to say modern time—completely organizes social existence and imposes itself upon the individual. The discipline of the industrial process has escaped the confines of the factory floor and dictates more and more of our timetable. Goodbye to the unforeseen, the unscheduled—the surprise.

To make matters worse, sleep experts have discovered that our natural sleep patterns vary from person to person, and just because you like to sleep late doesn't make you lazy and forcing yourself to wake up early is not going to make you more productive. People are genetically designed to be a "lark" (an early riser) or an "owl" (a late riser). If you want to be healthy and productive, you need to respect these differences and understand which one you are. Here is what Dr. Michael Breus, a sleep expert, has to say about it:

> Larks function best in the morning and tire through the day, whereas owls feel sharper as the day goes on and reach their optimum level at around 9:00 at night. Something else to keep in mind: not all "high-powered" people are early risers. Last year, scientists discovered that our skin cells may hold the clues to whether or not we are larks or owls. That's right: your internal clock may be pre-programmed to be an early riser or late-nighter. So don't mess with Mother Nature. Go to bed when you are tired, and get up when you are well-rested. Period.[ix]

For most of us, the idea of telling our bosses we'll be in at noon because we're "owls" is not an option. But if you *are* your boss, that's a different and much more exciting story. When you work the hours that align with your energy patterns, you will be happier and more productive. You work when your energy is up; rest when you are tired. Again, Thierry Paquot:

> Increasingly, city dwellers no longer work near their homes and cannot return there for a rest at siesta time, which is why those taking siestas tend not to be actively involved in full-time employment but are usually students, freelance travelers (ranging from the commercial to the more liberal professions, instructors, researchers, artists, or retired people: those who have, for good or ill, achieved control over their daily schedules.) This "privilege" is worth any raise in salary, providing as it does so many of the conditions for both physical and mental well-being.

Paquot is correct in valuing the privilege of the siesta, but I believe it can be available to full-time workers as well. I find time for a nap almost every day, because the only person I need approval from is myself. And Paquot is spot on regarding the health benefits of the siesta, according to Dr. Sara Mednick, author of *Take a Nap! Change Your Life*. She writes:

Imagine a product that increases alertness, boosts creativity, reduces stress, improves perception, stamina, motor skills, and accuracy, enhances your sex life, helps you make better decisions, keeps you looking younger, aids in weight loss, reduces the risk of heart attack, elevates your mood, and strengthens memory. Now imagine that this product is nontoxic, has no dangerous side effects, and, best of all, is absolutely *free.*[x]

The advantage of working for oneself is that there is never any need to kill time. You are only stealing from yourself, so why not be productive and then get on with something else? I go to my office, I work, I go home. I'm generally in around 9:30 a.m. and leave at 3:00 p.m. If we cut out the time used unproductively when working for others and following their rules, it is possible to complete a full day's work in five hours or less.[3] And Bohemians don't need to fill those extra hours with more work solely for the sake of more money—they have more important things to do.

The need to work our own schedule and to make our own rules is necessary for true satisfaction in our work environment. In his book, *Drive: The Surprising Truth About What Motivates Us,*[xi] Daniel Pink cites a study by Professor of Psychology Edward Deci and his colleague Richard Ryan, which found that autonomy is a human's most fundamental need, with "autonomy" being defined as *acting with choice.* It's hard to act with choice when you are punching somebody else's clock. In his book *Outliers: The Story of Success,*[xii] Malcolm Gladwell's research showed that autonomy, complexity, and a connection between effort and reward were the three qualities that work needed to provide in order to be fulfilling. He supported this claim with the example of the immigrant garment workers in New York City at the beginning of the 20th century. Despite working long hours doing hard tasks, they worked for themselves, piecemeal, and were forced to teach themselves marketing research, manufacturing, and negotiation skills. In telling one Polish immigrant's story, he wrote, "When Borgenicht came home at night to his children, he may have been tired and poor and overwhelmed, but he was alive. He was his own boss. He was responsible

---

3 The satirical newspaper *The Onion* ran a story on the amount of time people waste in the office with the headline: "48-Hour Internet Outage Plunges Nation into Productivity." As they say, it's funny because it's true.

for his own decisions and direction. His work was complex: it was a relationship between effort and reward." Writer and Bohemian Ann Powers agrees. She wrote, "More regular work, to be satisfying, must contain the capacity for play, which means some degree of independence and surprise."[xiii] We need to reevaluate what compensation encompasses. We must shift emphasis from money and benefits to autonomy and satisfaction, discover the appropriate balance, and then make it reality.

And, considering the changing nature of the workplace, it's best to be proactive about your future instead of living a life of anxiety waiting for the guillotine blade to drop. "America has entered the age of the contingent or temporary worker, of the consultant and subcontractor, of the just-in-time work force—fluid, flexible, disposable," writes *Time Magazine* and CNN journalist Lance Morrow.[xiv] "This is the future. Its message is this: you are on your own." But we've always been on our own when it comes to our life's purpose and our personal journey. The changing times are merely an opportunity, even if a brutal one, to wake up and be who we need to be on our own terms. In times of economic downturn, we tend to cling more tightly to our corporate jobs, and corporations take advantage of this neediness. They make sure we know how lucky we are to have the job and how easily we can be replaced, while increasing our workloads and responsibilities without increasing—and sometimes decreasing—salary and benefits, all so they can show record profits for shareholders. That's the ugly side of the free market.

But these are the times to engage that entrepreneurial spirit. When recently asked what he would most like to achieve professionally, a friend answered, "Employ a thousand people."[4] A worthy goal. I would tweak that and say I would like to inspire a thousand people to work for themselves. When we make this choice, support and encouragement can be found in like-minded souls. A friend of mine, a self-employed chair refurbisher, recently joined an "entrepreneurs collective," a group that gathers once a month to exchange information and ideas, and to barter and exchange services (i.e., website development for a refurbished chair). A great idea.

---

4 During the writing of this book, he achieved this benchmark.

But if, for whatever reason, you are unable to work for yourself, there is hope for you, too. Pink cites a growing trend of cutting-edge employers shifting to a "ROWE," an acronym for a Results Only Work Environment. "In a ROWE workplace, people don't have schedules," he writes. "They show up when they want. They don't have to be in the office at a certain time—or any time, for that matter. They just have to get their work done. How they do it, when they do it, and where they do it is up to them." This is a move in the right direction, and I encourage you to explore this with your employer. If you can't convince your boss to convert the whole office to a ROWE, then convince him or her to let you work once a week from home, then request two days a week, then three, and pretty soon you are back to being the manager of your life once again.[5]

And if you can't work for yourself, for a ROWE, or from home, what about job sharing? Doing a specific job twenty-five to thirty hours a week will result in less burnout and more diversity in our tasks. Yes, you will be cutting your pay in half and may lose certain benefits. But it is crucial we quantify how much money we actually need and how much time of our lives we're willing to sacrifice to get it. You may be surprised by how little is needed to satisfy your needs and to be happy.

If you choose to work part time or job share, then when you're not working your "regular job," you have time for another vocation, one that satisfies you in a way the other one doesn't. Work a half-week doing human relations at Big Money, Inc., and then work fifteen to twenty hours at the local independent bookstore, humane shelter or art museum.

Or, during the time you are not working, train yourself to do jobs that you would otherwise hire someone else to do for you. Stop paying a landscaper and take care of your own yard. Paint your own bedroom. Mend your own clothes and build your own deck chairs. Humans weren't meant to sit at a desk all day, every day, doing the same thing. Science fiction writer Robert Heinlein had little respect for those of us who master one skill

---

5 In Timothy Ferris's book, *The 4-Hour Work Week*, he offers an excellent strategy and script showing how to convince your employer that working from home is good for you and the company. Check it out and give it a try.

to the detriment of all others. "A human being should be able to change a diaper, plan an invasion, butcher a hog, conn a ship, design a building, write a sonnet, balance accounts, build a wall, set a bone, comfort the dying, take orders, give orders, cooperate, act alone, solve equations, analyze a new problem, pitch manure, program a computer, cook a tasty meal, fight efficiently, die gallantly," he wrote. "Specialization is for insects." I don't think I want him setting my bone, but he makes a good point.

It's important to remember that you do not have to dive in headfirst. Stick your toe in the water and ease in. Read books and blogs on consulting, entrepreneurship, and how to start a business. Take a seminar or join a class. Talk to those in your field (or the field you want to move into) who have already made the transition. I interviewed multiple solo practicing attorneys before I opened my office, learning the pros and cons and the minutiae such as what software to buy and where to go for office furniture. Moonlight at something you can do on your own while you still have a job and a paycheck so you can learn the ropes and determine whether the new field is really for you. Want to open a bar? Work as a barback first. You'll find out quickly if the dream matches the reality. The key is to be proactive.

But give up the excuses. Adam Baker, writer of the blog *Man Vs. Debt*, has talked with thousands of people struggling to change their lives and free themselves from debt, and he told me that the most common hurdle people have in achieving this success is the persistent need to focus on the reasons why they *can't*. "But until they look in the mirror and honestly say, 'I could do that if I wanted and I am choosing not to,' most people can't overcome their justifications," he told me. "So it becomes an impossibility even if they consciously say they want it."

The primary excuse I heard from people as to why they can't quit their corporate or institutional job to work for themselves was that they couldn't get by without the health insurance provided by their employer. They usually stop there, without having explored other options. For example, my health savings account allows me to deposit a certain amount each year, tax-free, to pay for my health costs. I have a $5,000 deductible, but I benefit by paying the vastly reduced rates that my insurance company has negotiated with my medical providers. I haven't met my deductible yet, but I have $5,000 set aside if a serious medical emergency arises. This plan costs me $113 a month. It's true, I don't suffer from serious health issues that others might, causing their monthly premiums to be higher. If you are in that situation, consider raising your deductible to $10,000, or $20,000 and work to set that money aside. If you're struggling to get individual coverage, many artisan, professional, or fraternal organizations provide group coverage. Join one of these.

After losing her job, a client of mine who is a cancer survivor was able to get health insurance with a $5,000 deductible with a $400 a month premium. She was shocked both that she was able to get this coverage and that the cost was reasonable. She decided to start the consulting business she had always wanted. Like many I talked to who resist leaving unhappy jobs, she had used the need for health insurance to prevent her from pursuing her dream without exploring other possibilities. Health concerns affect everyone differently, but spending your life working an unsatisfactory job so that you can be healthy enough to continue to live your life unhappily is crazy. Freedom in the precious time we have is more important than a security blanket, even a very real one.

The problem is, having health insurance is not a very safe security blanket. We are used to hearing horror stories from people being denied coverage for medicines, procedures, for "undisclosed" pre-existing conditions, and these stories come from people *with health insurance.* Private insurance is profit driven, and insurance companies have entire departments whose sole purpose is to figure out how to contractually and legally deny coverage to people who have been paying premiums for years. Another client of mine, fully insured by a major carrier through a plan with her large corporation, was diagnosed with cancer and after her insurance paid their obligations, she still owed $150,000. She was pushed into bankruptcy despite following the rules.

Of course, the Affordable Healthcare Act is reshaping the health insurance landscape. Regardless of whether we agree with the Act politically, it has opened up new avenues of healthcare coverage for the self-employed and otherwise uninsurable that did not exist before. It is difficult to predict whether the law will remain intact in its current form indefinitely, but as of January 2014, no less than nine million Americans have obtained health-care coverage, with the number estimated to be as high as fourteen million. To learn more, go to www.hhs.gov.

Finally, if you feel you can't leave an unhappy work situation because you need health insurance and can't get it on your own, ask yourself why that is, and then determine if you can do anything about it. Many of the health conditions we suffer from in the United States that cause coverage denial and/or result in expensive premiums, such as high blood pressure, type 2 diabetes, obesity, smoking, excessive alcohol and/or prescriptive drug abuse, acid reflux, sleep difficulties, etc., can be alleviated by proactive lifestyle changes. Not everything is within our control, but much is. It's not necessarily easy to make these changes, but neither is working forty to sixty hours at a miserable job. Getting rid of the excess stress caused by these unhappy jobs alone will make you healthier. When I worked for the firm, I compensated for my sleep deprivation by consuming caffeine and sugar, I suffered from stress-related acid reflux, and generally lived in a state of anxiety that I thought was just "life." That "life" and its dangerous side effects are gone. I no longer dread Monday mornings. Ask the tough questions and find the unconventional answers.

"The word liberty has no real meaning without each person having control over their own time," Thierry Paquot argues. I agree. If you need more proof, a poll of over 100,000 people taken in 2009 by the Gallup-Healthways Well-Being Index regarding work satisfaction found that people who work for themselves are the happiest and most fulfilled people, regardless of education.[xv] You will still have to work hard and be disciplined, but doing so won't feel like such a burden any more. But be careful to avoid the fate of Michael in John O'Farrell's novel, *The Best a Man Can Get*:

> I found it hard working really long hours when I was my own boss. The boss kept giving me the morning off as well. Sometimes he'd say, "Look, you've worked pretty hard today, why don't you take a well-earned rest tomorrow." If I overslept he never rang me to ask where I was; if

I was late to my desk he always happened to turn up at exactly the same time; whatever excuse I came up with, he always believed it. Being my own boss was great. Being my own employee was a disaster, but I never thought about that side of the equation.[xvi]

O'Farrell writes of this danger comically, but it is a very real one. When you work for yourself, only you can demand that you start work on time, that you be diligent and provide the services or products to your clients or customers as promised. Slacking off can be tempting, and working without supervision, often in solitude, can be daunting and intimidating. You will often need to learn new skills, such as office management, accounting, marketing, and budgeting. Create a circle of professionals in your field that can help you brainstorm issues and that you can go to when you need a second opinion. Learn how the wheel works before you try to reinvent it. Knowing you will reap the benefits of your labors instead of some faceless shareholder and that no superior will steal your credit should provide the incentive you need. The compensations that flow from doing your work well and on your own terms are many.

Take the middle path, my friends. "Do your work and then step back—it is the only path to serenity," advises Lao-Tzu. Don't work too much, but work enough. Having balance is good for the soul as well as the pocketbook. Wealth is not measured only in gold. Work for yourself, if possible, and if not, reclaim your freedom and control over your time as best you can. Remember, the goal is to find your Bohemian way and pay your bills at the same time. Small shifts in how we approach work can lead to expansive changes.

Open Yourself to Less Prestigious Jobs

One of the symptoms of an approaching nervous breakdown is the belief that one's work is terribly important.

Bertrand Russell

Kentuckian Silas House knew he wanted to be a novelist, but still had to buy groceries while he waited for success to come. He also knew he didn't want to hold a job that sucked all of his mental and creative energy away from his writing, so he took a job as a rural mail carrier. It paid the bills and the hours spent alone going house to house gave him time to think about his stories, and he still had energy at the end of the day to write. William Faulkner worked as a postmaster to support himself while writing, and Charles Bukowski also worked at the post office most of his life, during which he wrote dozens of popular novels, screenplays and poetry collections. Peter Matthiessen worked on a fishing boat, saved his money and dedicated the winter, the off-season, to his writing. In Van Morrison's song "Cleaning Windows," he sings of a man happily engaged in manual labor during the week, but blowing saxophone on the weekend, reading Jack Kerouac, and listening to blues records.

These artists knew who they were and what they wanted, and didn't let their egos compel them to need a so-called "prestigious" job.[6] Lofty titles and societal prestige are hard to give up when our self-esteem is determined by what we do instead of who we are. British philosopher Bertrand Russell didn't think our work was all that relevant in the big picture.

---

6 Throughout this book when I use the terms "creative expression" or "artist" I mean this expansively, to include all things in which we are passionately and actively engaged. It could be designing computer programs, running a social agency, or managing a doll factory as easily as painting or writing.

He said only two kinds of work existed: 1) moving bits of matter around at or near the surface of the earth; and 2) telling others to move bits of matter around at or near the surface of the earth. (I would add a third kind: moving digital bits through virtual space at or near the surface of the earth, and that would cover it.) Yet so much of how we define ourselves in our culture is based on how we make our money, regardless of what other gifts we have or how we otherwise spend our time. Other cultures don't necessarily view self-worth in the same way. The Balinese, for example, are much more interested in how a person chooses to express his or her authentic, creative side. Here is artist Corita Kent describing the Balinese:

> The Balinese have much to teach us about the (non) art of celebration. The making of splendid occasions occupies much of their time. If you ask a Balinese what he does, he will proudly answer, "I am a Baris Dancer" or "I am a mask maker." If you persist and ask again, "No, I mean how do you get your rice?" he loses interest, his voice drops, he may turn away, deciding this is a pretty boring conversation. "Oh, that," he will say.[xvii]

To be successful at something doesn't mean you have to make money doing it. And sometimes the pressure to achieve financial reward from our art can hinder our development. The desire for commercial success has caused many talented people to compromise their true vision in the hope they will make more money if they match what (they perceive) the market wants. I would love to have the audience and commercial success of author John Grisham, but I have no interest in legal thrillers and that would be evident in my writing. The fraudulence would show through. When you don't rely on your art to pay the rent, you are less likely to be seduced by this temptation. And frankly, I have a lot more respect for those who work less glamorous jobs, saving their true gifts for their passion, but still earn their own way and maintain their independence. The rewards are that much sweeter when they come. "To depend upon a profession is a less odious form of slavery than to depend upon a father," Virginia Woolf said. This concept sticks in the craw of those of us who are college educated and middle class. We were taught we need a career, and if we didn't have one, well, what were we? Certainly not ambitious. Without career we lack direction;

we lack purpose. Success requires credentials, degrees, promotions and titles. We read the autobiographies of industrial tycoons and ex-presidents, not kindergarten teachers or hospice workers, after all. In *What Can You Do With a Law Degree,*[xviii] former lawyer Deborah Arron writes that one of the most difficult hurdles to overcome when moving from the legal field to a different line of work is letting go of the "prestige" that comes with being an attorney. I acknowledge I experienced this fear, and it troubled me to discover how much my self-worth was wrapped up in my job. That gave me cause for serious self-analysis.

Numerous examples can be found of talented and prolific artists who paid their bills by working "un-Bohemian" jobs. I included the photograph of Hemingway wearing a beret and sitting in the Spanish Café at the beginning of the book because that scene typifies what being "Bohemian" means to most of us. But Hemingway was no fool. He got a job as a foreign correspondent with the Toronto Daily Star *before* he moved to Paris. He and his wife, Hadley, wanted to live like Bohemians, "So they moved into an apartment in the Latin Quarter in a neighborhood full of drunks and beggars and street musicians."[xix] Hemingway may have lived with beggars, but he was making good money. His rent was only eighteen dollars a month, and they used the rest of his salary to travel Europe. Make good money, live cheaply, travel a lot. That's living unconventionally.

Although John Prine may have been speaking mockingly of insurance jobs in his song, "Illegal Smile, " when he sang, "all my friends turned out to be insurance salesmen," the industry has supported a surprising number of creative folk. Poet Wallace Stevens, winner of both the Pulitzer Prize and National Book Award, was president of an insurance company most of his life. Former U.S. Poet Laureate Ted Kooser worked for the Lincoln Benefit Company until he was sixty, becoming vice-president along the way. But every morning he got up at dawn and wrote poetry before going to work. Compared to many, he is a slow writer, and has said he is happy if he produces a dozen poems he feels are worthwhile in a year. But as with the race-winning tortoise, that diligence pays off. He published a dozen books of poetry over his career and after retiring from the insurance company he became a professor of poetry. He continues writing in the early mornings. And perhaps the most famous of insurance industry-supported artists, Franz Kafka was a dedicated employee of the Worker's Accident Insurance Institute in Prague. He worked there for fourteen years figuring out compensation for injured workers.

Wallace Stevens personifies the idea of living an unconventional life without starving perhaps more than anyone. After attending Harvard Law School, he worked as a journalist, a lawyer, and then became vice-president of the Hartford Insurance Company, a job he maintained the rest of his life. On the surface, you don't get much more conventional than that. But Wallace walked to and from work every day, and on these walks he wrote poems, publishing a dozen books of poetry during his life as well as numerous collections of essays and letters. His poetry is recognized and respected, and he didn't have to live in a refrigerator box in a New York back alley to create it. Often when a person describes his or her profession we tend to project certain traits onto them while denying them others. We do this to ourselves as well, denying talents and passions because we have chosen to wear one label and don't believe we can have two. Or three. Or a dozen. So when someone (including the inner, fearful you) tries to tell you that you can't be a singer and an actuary, or a sculptor and a Rotary Club Member, remember Wallace Stevens and know that you can wear all the hats you want. Don't pigeon-hole yourself and don't pigeon-hole others either.

I've certainly been guilty of prematurely judging others. At a neighborhood party I met an engineer and after talking to him a few moments I decided that he was nice enough, but ultimately not very interesting. He was quiet, content to be in the background, and certainly looked the part of a left-brained math and science type. I assumed his interest in the arts stopped with *Star Trek*. A few weeks later at a PechaKucha[7] event I was shown how wrong my assessment was. A passionate gourd artist, he presented to the crowd an array of amazing tribal animal masks that he

---

7 Started in Tokyo, A PechaKucha is an informal gathering for creative types to share their ideas and work. The gatherings are now happening in over 230 cities around the world. I highly encourage you to attend and participate. They're fun.

had sculpted, carved and painted for a local school play. Monkeys, lions, birds—the masks were beautiful. He was animated and engaging, showing a side that I hadn't seen at the party and therefore assumed didn't exist. If I had been more open and inquisitive when we first met, I probably would have learned about his art and would have left inspired and a bit wiser about making quick judgments. I learned the lesson.

In *The Yoga of Work*, writer Rick Jarow distinguishes one's "job" from one's "vocation."[xx] Vocation is your passion, your life purpose. Your job is what supports your vocation. They can be the same thing, but often they are not. "Is that what they call a vocation, what you do with joy as if you had fire in your heart, the devil in your body?" Josephine Baker once asked. Yes, Miss Baker. It is. Jarow writes that as long as we "honor the energies that are guiding us toward our vocational destinies," the way you make your money doesn't really matter. Sometimes it is best to take a job that pays your bills but doesn't drain your creative energy away from your true calling. Doing so will remove the pressure of "success" and that is the path to freedom.

We must get past the notion that purity of art and bourgeois means of making money are irreconcilable. If you can make the money from your gift, then do so. If you can't make enough from your gift, find something else to support you materially and let your gift support you in other ways.

Hardship and Progress

He who has a why to live can bear almost any how.

Friedrich Nietzsche

Odysseus, star of two of the greatest adventure stories of all time, didn't want to fight in the Trojan War (he pretended to be crazy to get out of it) but made a pretty good showing of himself once he got there. It was his idea to sneak the wooden horse inside the city enabling the Achaeans to win the war. All in all, he did what was asked of him and when the war ended he just wanted to go home. But the Gods, alas, had other ideas and kept him from reaching home until ten years after the war ended. During this time his ships were destroyed, his men turned into pigs, the Cyclops almost had him for dinner, and when he was within sight of his home in Ithaca, the winds blew his ship back to where he started. Talk about frustration.

Everyone knows of *The Odyssey*, Odysseus's story. Why? Because myths are metaphors for our own lives; they speak to us because they contain universal truths about what it means to live in this world, and *The Odyssey* more than most. Sometimes, despite your best efforts, the stars align to make success seem impossible despite knowing in the depths of your heart that you are on the right path. That is the time to buck up and endure. Don't be afraid of a little hardship. If you're moving forward, whether it is creatively, spiritually or financially, stick with it. Don't quit until you know (as opposed to fear deceiving you) that it is time to change directions. Henry Miller was forty when he moved to Paris with only three sub-par unpublished novels under his belt to remind himself he was a writer. He had a hard time in Paris for a while but things got better, and the rough times inspired *Tropic of Cancer*. His father was a tailor and he wanted Henry to take over the family business and he probably would have led a comfortable life had he done so. But that was not his life purpose. He borrowed money to pay for the passage from New York to London and arrived with only ten dollars in his pocket. He moved to Paris where he struggled initially, relying on help from friends and living a meager existence. He convinced seven separate friends to give him one meal a week, thus guaranteeing he would have at least one meal a day while he struggled to pay his bills. He eventually landed a job working at a newspaper spot-checking stock prices while he worked on *Tropic of Cancer*. He met the writer Anaïs Nin, who became his patron and lover. He found success with his writing, living life on his own terms: roaming the streets and cafés of Paris, making love to Anaïs, writing novels, and generally living life to the fullest.

You may think, "But I can't ask others for help. That would be taking advantage of them and my pride won't let me." Maybe. Maybe not. Henry Miller acknowledged the difficulty of relying on handouts from others when he needed them (a brief time period in the span of his life). But the people who helped him received gifts in return. When he became famous, they relished the fact that they had a part in his success. Some of them, Anaïs being the most notable, wrote books about the time spent with Henry and achieved fame and fortune as well. Even before his success, many of his patrons felt he compensated them with his wit and personality at their dinner tables. But he had to wait until he was seventy, when the ban on *Tropic of Cancer* was lifted and it could be sold in the United States, to make any real money from it. His response? "The thing is, never to be too anxious. Everything comes in due time."

The suffering, paradoxically, can be part of the pleasure. No one knows how wonderful water tastes more than the man who just dragged himself through the desert. There is no light without darkness. The insight you can obtain from your hardship can shift your experience from suffering to inspiration. I'd prefer to read about Jack Kerouac sleeping in a barn with a Mexican señorita than about him getting room service at the Hilton. While writing *One Hundred Years of Solitude,* Gabriel Garcia Marquez lived off his life savings and when that ran out, his wife sold piece by piece their household items—their blender, their coffee pot, their utensils—to pay their meager bills so he could finish. That is hard, that is scary, and that is brave. That shows belief. Do you have that belief? Then stick with it. If not, surround yourself with people who will believe for you...until you do. It is important to note that Marquez's wife was in it with him, sharing his belief and his struggles. It was she who sold one of the last remaining household items they had in order to buy the postage to mail his manuscript to the publisher. So many of us have people who believe in us, love us, and are willing to help us along if they see the authenticity of our passion and commitment. Trust them. Allow them to help, and then don't let them down. That doesn't mean you guarantee them you will obtain material success; only that you commit not to quit. You commit to live your bliss. If you do, they won't be disappointed. "If you follow your bliss, you will always have your bliss; if you follow money, you may lose it sometime," advised Joseph Campbell. And he walked the talk. In the introduction to *An Open Life*, Michael Toms writes of Campbell:

His early years proved to Joseph that he could do whatever he wanted to do without having to be a slave to money—one of the characteristics associated with those courageous enough to follow their bliss as he did. Living on very little, making himself easily available as a dinner guest, and freelancing sometimes as a jazz musician, Joseph was able to spend long periods of time simply reading—all the while mining the treasure trove of knowledge which later became available to us all through his prolific writing.[xxi]

In our instant-gratification society, patience is scarce. We don't want to wait for anything, success or otherwise. "A creative life is grounded on many, many small steps and very, very few large leaps," writes Julia Cameron. It's much easier to fail quickly than to march the long walk to success. But we sacrifice so much with our constant haste. I love this beautiful passage from Basil, Zorba's boss:

I remembered one morning when I discovered a cocoon in the bark of a tree, just as the butterfly was making a hole in its case and preparing to come out. I waited a while, but it was too long appearing and I was impatient. I bent over it and breathed on it to warm it. I warmed it as quickly as I could and the miracle began to happen before my eyes, faster than life. The case opened, the butterfly started slowly crawling out and I shall never forget my horror when I saw how its wings were folded back and crumbled; the wretched butterfly tried with its whole trembling body to unfold them. Bending over it, I tried to help it with my breath. In vain. It needed to be hatched out patiently and the unfolding of the wings should be a gradual process in the sun. Now it was too late. My breath had forced the butterfly to appear, all crumpled, before its time. It struggled desperately and, a few seconds later, died in the palm of my hand.

That little body is, I do believe, the greatest weight I have on my conscience. For I realize today that it is a mortal sin to violate the great laws of nature. We should not hurry, we should not be impatient, but we should confidently obey the eternal rhythm.

It's too bad Basil didn't follow Anne Morrow Lindbergh's advice. Being patient is difficult but seldom fails to reward. Using the sea as a metaphor, Lindbergh writes:

The sea does not award those who are too anxious, too greedy, or too impatient. To dig for treasures shows not only impatience and greed, but lack of faith. Patience, patience, patience, is what the sea teaches. Patience and faith. One should lie empty, open, choiceless as a beach—waiting for a gift from the sea.[xxii]

Move slowly, but keep moving. At a conference I met a writer who wrote nine novels before having one accepted by a publishing house. *Nine novels.* That's patience and that's faith. I don't know if I have that resilience, but I hope I do, and I hope you do, too. Cut yourself a break and just do today's job today. That is success enough.

So you are willing to take risks and let go of the illusion of security. You understand and accept that there will most likely be times of hardship, and success requires patience. But this acceptance alone won't prevent struggle, stress and self-doubt. You will question your decisions and will recriminate yourself. But if you are engaged and believe in your work, start with *self-faith* and move forward. When musician Patti Smith and photographer Robert Mapplethorpe were struggling for artistic recognition in their early years in New York, Patti relied on her faith that what they were doing was meaningful and that someday their art would be celebrated. "We were like fishermen throwing out our nets," she wrote about their experience.[xxiii] "The net was strong but often we returned empty-handed." Have faith that you, too, have woven strong nets.

The people who have spurned their true purpose in order to make money or to feed their security illusion face the same problems, only when the bad times hit, they will have the additional layer of suffering caused by having lived an inauthentic life. A friend of mine works in an accounting department of a large corporation, and is one of the first to know when a round of layoffs is coming, and they come often. She is privy to a list of people that show up to work every day, comforted by their secure position, but won't have a job in a few short weeks. This knowledge causes her much stress and anxiety and she feels compassion for them, as do I. I don't envy her position and I'm glad I'm not one of the people waiting to know if his or her name is on the cutting board. You don't want to be one of them either.

When one struggles for money, it's not fun. But we can take advantage of this struggle instead of being consumed with worry and stress. Use the downtimes for reflection, as a time for exploring the joys and happiness found in the things money can't buy. Can't afford to go to the movies? Fine. Go for a walk in the woods instead. Use that free time to paint, write, dance. Use the lack of money as motivation to delve deeper into your art and deeper into yourself. Money struggles can really damage our egos. But that can be a good thing: many illusions we have constructed about ourselves can be stripped away. Use this time of struggle to refocus your vision. And lack of money can be freeing, at least to Henry Miller. "I have no money, no resources, no hopes. I am the happiest man alive," he wrote. Use that as your mantra through the tough times. Seek pleasure and solace in the small, the inexpensive, and the intangible and free beauty that surrounds us. During her period of struggle Patti Smith made a ritual of going to a deserted beach café every Sunday for coffee and a donut. "I savored these small indulgences, slipping a quarter in the jukebox and listening to 'Strawberry Fields' three times in a row," she wrote of the experience. "It was a private ritual and the words and voice of John Lennon provided me with strength when I faltered." Small indulgences are often all that is needed. "Happiness is a simple, unaffected thing: a glass of wine, a chestnut, a humble little brazier, the roar of the sea," wrote Nikos Kazantzakis.

To Nikos' list I would add a good book and a hammock and you've got a formula for cheap bliss. And science is beginning to prove that inexpensive bliss is, essentially, the only bliss. Dr. Richard Tunney of the University of Nottingham in the U.K. conducted a recent study in which the happiness levels of lottery winners were tracked and compared with a control group and he found that purchases of *things*, both the elaborately expensive such as sports cars and high-end jewelry, as well as the mildly expensive, such as DVDs and shoes, gave a temporary high but no long lasting joy. However, the study found that non-expensive, *experiential* activities, such as listening to music, reading, napping or taking a walk provide sustaining, lasting happiness.[xxiv] "Cost-free pleasures are the ones that make the difference—even when you can afford anything that you want," Tunney said.

Practice the art of detachment. Repeat this Jamaican proverb to find the bright side of difficult times: "If you are sick, don't worry. Either you get better or you die. If you get better, you are happy. But if you die, you still shouldn't worry. You either go to Heaven or go to Hell. If you go to Heaven, you are happy. If you go to Hell, you still shouldn't worry: you will be with all your friends. Either way you are happy!"

And the lack of money is seldom a true reason to veer away from your life's true journey. As spiritual coach and author David Deida writes, "Limited money and family obligations have never stopped a man who *really* wanted to do something, although they provide excuses for a man who is not really up to the creative challenge in the first place."[xxv] Julia Cameron agrees. "All too often, we become blocked and blame it on our lack of money," she writes. "This is never an authentic block. The actual block is our feeling of constriction, our sense of powerlessness."[xxvi] Use the lack of money as a spur, not a bridle. Get out there and do. You'll prove yourself to yourself in ways that people who never lacked money are not able to do. Here is the brilliant and blunt writer Nick Tosches' take on those who never faced money struggles:

> Fuck you people with your paid vacations and your pensions and your rich mommies and daddies and your bullshit about how hard you work and how much you sacrifice . . . I hate every

49

one of you motherfuckers who ever inherited a dime, or who stands to inherit a dime. You're the scum of the earth, because you can't make your own way on it. Even if you pretend to make your own way, you've got that net under you. You're dilettantes of real life.[xxvii]

Strong words, but they carry the ring of truth. When the money does come back—and if you stay true to your purpose, I believe it will—you can have the pride that you traveled to the River Styx and returned to the world of the sun with your soul expanded. That's no small thing.

And what happens when the struggle ends? What if you are in a position where you don't need to struggle to begin with? Then you have different challenges to face. If you have work that pays well and you are not sacrificing your passions or the time necessary to pursue your true calling, why stop? If you feel challenged or guilty because of your material wealth, the cause may be due to an unrealistic view of what it means to have integrity. Most early-stage Bohemians view anything bourgeois as the enemy, and never shall the twain meet. Wealth and material success is the province of the greedy capitalists and those pure of heart must reject such wants at all costs. If you find this an unnecessary and unrealistic simplification you are correct, but you may be surprised at the number of us who struggle with this very concept, even if unconsciously. Sometimes our financial struggles are self-inflicted but there are simple ways to change this mindset.

Money coach[8] Nakia Angelique counsels holistic health practitioners and artists on how to improve their relationship with commerce. "Holistic health practitioners" include massage therapists, bodyworkers, yoga instructors, Reiki practitioners, and so on. Her clientele are typically women who prioritize the needs of others above their own. They are over-givers and under-receivers. They often believe their skill is a spiritual gift that God or the universe has bestowed upon them, that they "get" to use this gift and they have a duty to provide it to others even if others can't pay them for it. They are apt to give their services away or not charge a high enough rate. They don't feel comfortable marketing themselves because market-

---

8 A "money coach" is someone trained to help people become more comfortable with capitalistic exchange and how to properly monetize the services they offer.

ing is too "sales-y" and to advertise means you are dissatisfied and greedy. Marketing is bragging. The Universe will provide, they tell themselves, but making good money feels excessive. If they earn more than what is required to meet their basic needs, they must be taking from someone who doesn't have enough. They feel guilty if they are not suffering, as if they are not being empathetic to those who are. Gandhi suffered; therefore I must, too.

"My clients experience a disconnection between the spiritual world and the material world," Angelique said. Success bears hurdles enough without shackling ourselves with such unnecessary weight. Ironically, this school of thought causes the outside world to devalue the worth of what these people have to offer. "When the practitioners I advise give away or discount their services, their clients miss appointments, they show up late, they're erratic. When they raise their rates, people fall in line. It's about the perception of value." So how do we reconcile material wealth with a spiritually pure soul?

Angelique counsels these folks to understand that when we are living and experiencing fully, we can give more to others. "The more you have, the more you have to give back to the world," she tells them. "Money is a tool; a form of energy. View yourself as a channel for that tool. Yes, it's a gift to have a talent, and it's a gift to be shared, but it's your financial resource, also. To say that you don't need to be paid for what you do is to deny part of the gift. We need people with these gifts to have an impact on the world and to support worthwhile causes financially. And it's fun, and okay, to be a hedonist every once in a while, too." You can save the world and buy those expensive new shoes if they make you happy.

Dayton, Ohio bodyworker Marianne Fink has found this balance. In fact, she says, it's never really been a struggle during her thirteen years working in the field. Like Angelique, she views money as merely the form in which we exchange energy in our culture, and is not to be feared or viewed as ugly or profane. Bodywork is her calling, her gift, and she knows her value. She's *good* at what she does, and she doesn't question that. Having this attitude and an ability to be present and completely engaged with the energy of the moment, as much as the physical work itself, allows her to connect with her clients in a deeper way. And when they experience this fullness, they recognize its worth and are willing to pay for it. With few exceptions, she feels she benefits from this exchange as much as her clients do.

She believes in the law of attraction, but applies it in a very practical way: heart open, mind grounded. "I understand that when a new body-worker starts practicing they feel a need to discount their work, but I think this scarcity mentality is counterproductive," she said. "Discounting shows a lack of belief in the value of what you can do, that you doubt the importance of your profession and what you can offer. If you don't believe in it, why should your clients? Become good at what you do and be present and engaged with the person and the value will be recognized. Even in situations that don't start off well, you can find that connection and break through with the client. And they will experience this and they will come back. And they will pay you what it's worth." Whether you believe success comes from positive thinking, spiritual attraction, hard work or all of the above, confidence, belief, presence and commitment must be present. Just as Marianne knows the value of what she does and is comfortable with getting paid well for it, she enjoys exchanging the money back to others for the gifts they can provide her.

You can substitute lawyer, photographer or landscaper for body-worker, and the same rules apply. I struggled with discounting my own work as a young lawyer and would lose confidence when a client expressed surprise at "how expensive" my services were. I quickly discovered that for every sticker-shocked client, another client would reply, "Is that all?" when quoted the same price. I learned I couldn't control others' expectations. But I could control the quality of my work and my own belief in its value. It's okay to let some clients or customers go so others who understand your value can take their place.

Being comfortable with charging the full worth of her services doesn't mean Marianne refuses to offer her services for a different price or different exchange or even for free if she sees a need and has the power to fill that need. But that choice is based on compassion, not from guilt or fear caused by someone undermining her value.

I had the opportunity to exercise this balance recently when a client called me on a Friday morning and told me about a tragedy that happened to her friend, Laura.[9] Laura's son was hit by a speeding police car while crossing the street. His back was broken in multiple places, he suffered severe head trauma and was in a coma. People had rallied to support him and his family and were donating money to help with medical bills piling up from the intensive care required. The family needed a trust created to hold these funds, but didn't have the money to pay for the legal work. After hearing the story, I stopped what I was doing, drafted the documents needed, and met Laura at the hospital to complete it. I admit at first I agreed to do the work because I didn't know how to say no, but when I met with Laura and her family, saw the impact I had on her and how appreciative she was, I was deeply moved and felt really good about my choice. The compensation I received was more than any amount of money could have provided, and it reminded me of the value of doing *a good thing*. It's a lesson I won't forget soon. On Monday, I went back to billing for my work.

Many artists and healers struggle with material success, but they are not alone. Hal Hansen, CEO of Denver-based Energie, LLC, spent more than thirty years consulting entrepreneurs and multimillion-dollar companies. In doing this, he found three hurdles that consistently limit a person's success. First: social stigma. Believing that you will lose the connection you have with your family, friends and community. Fear that others will view you as a snobby elitist and you will be ostracized from your social circle. Second: if others see you as having money, they will want something from you. People will begin demanding things, expecting things. Better not to have it at all. Third: fear of losing it, that the level of success cannot be reached again, cannot be repeated. The only way to go is down. Speaking at a TED[10] conference in 2009, writer Elizabeth Gilbert admitted she experienced this fear following the mega-success of *Eat, Pray, Love*. Everywhere

---

9 Not her real name.
10 The nonprofit TED, short for Technology, Entertainment and Design, hosts annual conferences for "thinkers and doers" to share public talks. Check them out at TED.com. It's worth it.

Joseph Downing

she went people treated her like she was doomed. "Aren't you afraid you won't be able to top that?" she was asked. "Aren't you afraid you are going to keep writing for your whole life and you're never again going to create a book that anybody in the world cares about at all, ever again?" And she admitted she was afraid of these things. But she learned to get over it. She decided to go back to the original Greek definition of "genius," which was not something you *were*, but something outside of you that *flowed through* you. A separate entity, or being, that chose you as the vehicle to bring it into the world. Therefore, if you create something great, you can't claim full credit; but if your creation fails, it isn't entirely your fault, either.

It's natural to want to improve, to grow, to expand, to welcome wealth and abundance, but it's easier said than done. It can be more comfortable to fail than to succeed, Hansen said, because growth requires change, and people are resistant to change. "People don't want to believe they could be fundamentally wrong in their perspective," he said. "I try to accentuate their discomfort, get them to describe their perfect world. To see it, taste it, touch it, smell it with absolute clarity. Then write it down. Verbalize it. Visualize it. Understand that the discomfort they feel is good—it acknowledges you are ready to move to someplace new." He then helps them bridge the gap from their current reality to the new world they want, step by small step.

Whether you are an acupuncturist or web designer, doula or marketing director, accept the fear. Listen to the discomfort. Let it guide you to a new place and accept willingly and thankfully the gifts, both spiritual and material, your work brings to you.

Make a living, Bohemians, but also make your art. Embrace the struggles along the way and equally embrace the material rewards when they come. Don't be afraid of money. Just don't make it the most important thing.

Turn Your Suffering into Inspiration

Forget your personal tragedy. We are all bitched from the start and you especially have to be hurt like hell before you can write seriously. But when you get the damned hurt, use it-don't cheat with it.

Ernest Hemingway

A high station in life is earned by the gallantry with which appalling experiences are survived with grace.

Tennessee Williams

When Frida Kahlo was eighteen, a trolley car broadsided the bus in which she was riding. In the horrific collision, Frida's spine, pelvis and collarbone were fractured. Her right leg was broken in eleven places. Her shoulder and foot were dislocated. An iron rod penetrated her abdomen and uterus. "By rights you should be dead," her doctors told her.[xxviii] They also told her she might never walk again. She lay for months in the hospital on her back, strapped to a board, encased in a plaster cast. What did she do? Despite having no training or previous experience, she asked for paints, brushes, and an easel to stand within reach of her arms, the only mobile part of her body. "She underwent a profound metamorphosis in character," Bertram Wolfe wrote. "It is questionable whether the painter known as Frida Kahlo would have existed were it not for that year of suffering and constraint."

When something bad happens to us, the pain can be so great that we think our life is over. But this pain can also be a catalyst to discover new aspects of ourselves. It can cause us to change the way we live, to change jobs or careers, or to reevaluate priorities. The raw feelings and intense experience allow us to delve into areas with our art that brings out our best, as it did with Kahlo.

55

When Hermann Hesse's marriage ended, he suffered a nervous breakdown. Following this, he wrote his most famous novel, *Siddhartha*, which upon its release only attracted modest attention. But, forty years later and in a span of ten years, fifteen million copies of his works were sold in the U.S. alone. And like Hesse, you may have to be patient to reap your rewards. In a world of instant gratification, this is difficult to do. We may have the same fate as Herman Melville, who died in obscurity with *Moby-Dick* out of print and deemed a failure. Only later was it recognized as one of America's greatest novels. Sometimes even success feels like failure if we don't meet the expectations we set for ourselves. After Orville and Wilbur Wright conducted their first flight at Kitty Hawk, they were deeply disappointed with the result. Wilbur said, "Not within a thousand years will man ever fly." Two men changed the world that day, and still it was not enough.

Alas, it is the nature of the Bohemian to suffer from time to time (it is the nature of human beings to suffer from time to time), and many of our greatest works of art, art that has comforted, informed and inspired us has come from that suffering. Respect your suffering; you suffer because you feel. You suffer because you take risks, you love, and you don't hide from the world. Dissatisfaction and pain can propel us forward, or it can cause us to wallow and withdraw. You can step away, grieve, rage and regret. That's part of the human experience, too. But come back and use your experience.

Use your suffering for inspiration not only for the creative beauty it helps bring to yourself and others. Don't discard this gift by wallowing in resentment, self-pity and self-doubt. Sadly, too many of us make the second choice. John Kennedy Toole, author of *A Confederacy of Dunces*, is a tragic example. When he couldn't get his novel published, he committed suicide in despair. His mother kept working to find a publisher for it and when she did, it won the Pulitzer Prize and is considered a classic today, still read widely. It's a favorite of mine. I wish he had endured to leave us more of his wonderful art, but more importantly, to realize that his life is worth more than a publisher's opinion.

If only he had followed the path of the architect Buckminster Fuller.

The Abundant Bohemian

By the age of thirty-two, he was jobless, living in low-income housing, and had filed bankruptcy. When his daughter died of complications related to polio and spinal meningitis, he considered committing suicide. He pulled himself back from the edge and decided to conduct "an experiment . . . to find what a single individual can contribute to changing the world and benefiting all of humanity." He became one of America's most celebrated architects, and was awarded the Presidential Medal of Freedom and the Humanist of the Year award among many other achievements. Ford Maddox Ford's life provides another good example. At age forty-one he suffered from depression and financial debt. He used this time of struggle to gain the experiences needed to write *A Good Soldier*, a classic that is considered his best novel.

Charles Schulz always wanted to be a cartoonist, but he struggled in school, was bullied by students and teachers, and his mother died young from cancer. And perhaps most significantly, his heart was broken when the red-haired Donna Mae Johnson rejected his marriage proposal only to accept the offer of another man. But he took his heartbreak and compassionate world-weariness and filtered it through *Peanuts* and touched the hearts of millions for over fifty years. We can all relate to the unrequited love Charlie Brown felt for the little red-haired girl.

Looking back at the fiction I wrote in my early twenties I can find evidence of my potential as a writer, but most of it feels more clever than substantial. I wasn't offering the reader much. Only after I experienced my own personal suffering was I able to tap into that deeper, more vulnerable place within myself and give readers something of value that was able to touch them emotionally. When my mother died of cancer at age fifty-eight, I was able to channel my pain and sorrow into a short story that readers responded to strongly and was honored by being published in *Best of Ohio Short Stories: Vol. 1*. I'm very proud of that story, and only through my suffering was I able to write it. And writing it was cathartic, too.

And one need not use one's suffering only to create for the outer world; sometimes it is enough for our suffering to be a catalyst for personal, inner change. A friend of mine survived a heart attack several years ago,

57

and this near-death experience awoke him to the beauty and fragility of life in a way nothing previously had, and he now has an ability to savor, appreciate and live in the moment beyond what many of us have achieved. To him, every moment seems like a gift, that he really shouldn't be here any more, and that heightens his awareness of the awesome beauty that is life.

If you live fully, you will suffer. But difficult times test the depth of your inner strength, and the measure of that depth is a valuable thing to know. You are more resilient than you think. Use your pain. Don't escape it, delve into it. You will feel raw but you will feel alive.

Reevaluate Where You Live

A community needs a soul if it is to become a true home for human beings. You, the people, must gift it this soul.

Pope John Paul II

No matter where you live, someone is going to say that it is not authentic, that it is dead, that it is not like it used to be. You can't live *here* and be Bohemian; you must live *there*. Don't buy into it. Bohemia is where you make it.

After having been gone for many years, journalist and author Emily Hahn returned to Greenwich Village to visit the "haunts of her youth" and to see what had become of her Bohemian Mecca. She was disappointed. The young "carelessly and lightly dressed" characters hanging around with "no apparent errands" bothered her. "It wasn't a bit like this in my day," she wrote. Something was missing. It was no longer the Bohemia she knew.

This was in 1964. Bob Dylan was just settling in at the Village.

Here is how she described what she witnessed:

> Streets resounding with music from guitars and accordions played on street corners or indoors. Blaring theme songs from a movie palace. Pale girls with long streaky hair and tight black pants, kids carrying books, kids carrying musical instruments . . . Black and white couples were big in the Village.

I beg to disagree, Ms. Hahn. That sounds just like Bohemia to me. But, little did she know, the Village was long dead before the time she looked back upon with nostalgia. In *Garrets and Pretenders, a History of Bohemians in America*, Albert Parry reported that in the 1920s and 30s "true" Bohemians held the opinion that Greenwich Village had been taken over by "Babbittry," a term derived from Upton Sinclair's novel *Babbitt* and used to mockingly describe the bourgeoisie. "By 1927, thanks to this invasion, the word was wide and firm that the Village was nothing but bogus and a lewd bore," he wrote. And apparently, the Latin Quarter in Paris suffered the same early demise. Parry writes:

> In 1878, the eighteen-year-old James Huneker was aggrieved in Paris. He could not find the genuine gaiety and intellect of the Latin Quarter! There was no Latin Quarter in Paris! In vain he circled around Paris looking for the glorious spot. "An old Frenchman informed me," wrote Jim, "that Paris had seen the last of the famous Quarter after the Commune, but a still older person swore that the Latin Quarter had not been in existence since 1848.

This was seventy years before Ford Maddox Ford, Ezra Pound, Hemingway, Gertrude Stein, James Joyce, T.S. Eliot, Henry Miller, Picasso, Josephine Baker and Vladimir Nabokov moved to the Latin Quarter. Someone should have told them of Mr. Huneker's opinion and saved them the bother of showing up. And I believe Ms. Hahn was sincere in that, for her, Greenwich Village was no longer the Bohemia she had known and therefore no longer attracted her. However, for many others living there, Bohemia was just unfolding.

Because the cost of living is a major obstacle to living the Bohemian life, Bohemia is most often found where living is cheap. Many of us who choose to live in "glamorous" places end up having to work so hard to meet the bare minimum of our living needs that we have little energy left to practice our art or to enjoy the benefits of our chosen locale. A friend of mine who is a talented fashion designer lives in Brooklyn and loves it. However, she works such long hours as a waitress to pay for her two-bedroom apartment that she shares with a roommate that she has little time to spend on her designs. That works for her, but I couldn't do it. I love New York, San Francisco and L.A. and am happy every time I have a chance to visit, but I don't need to live there.

The key is to find a place that strikes a balance between supporting your passion while not draining you of your life energy with excessive expenses. Smaller cities tend to allow us to do just that. Places like Austin (recently named the best place in the United States to see live music), Portland, Denver (where residents contribute more per capita to the arts than any other city in the United States) and Columbus are a few examples. Legitimate business and artistic reasons to be in places like New York, L.A. or London exists, of course, but snobbish pride is not one of them. If you fall into that category, reevaluate. If living in a vibrant, supportive, Bohemian culture is your goal, expand your possibilities and open your eyes—these communities exist everywhere.

Take my humble town of Dayton, Ohio. Few would note it on the artistic map, but those willing to look will find a vibrant and energized artistic community flourishing here. The cost of living is cheap and talented people have time to create beautiful things. Several of these artists I discuss in this book. When bores say, "Nothing's happening here," or "Dayton is dead," I shake my head and want to scream at them to look around. Perhaps you hear similar comments about your city. Don't give into it. Usually these people aren't bored with their town, they're bored with themselves. "For a Bohemian the parental home, no matter where it is, invariably falls short of the ideal," Emily Hahn wrote. That is true, and it is a false prejudice. Keep this in mind and look at your locale with fresh eyes.

And if you feel uninspired or unsupported where you live, instead of changing towns, consider making a change in your town. Start a revolution in your backyard. That's what Hamilton and Carli Dixon did in Dayton.

Hamilton is a well-recognized metal sculptor. He sculpted the beautiful railings that line the staircase at the Dayton Art Institute and the lobby of the Dayton International Airport, among his many other works. Carli is an artist and an entrepreneur who, with her mother, started a flower preservation and jewelry business that still thrives today. When I met with Hamilton at his studio it was with the purpose of talking about his metal sculpture, but the conversation quickly turned to how he and Carli were sculpting the city of Dayton into a place they wanted it to be.

Hamilton needed a new studio space and when he and Carli were driving through the city one day, she suggested they check out an abandoned building on 3rd Street downtown. Hamilton was skeptical, but Carli insisted. They climbed the railing and peered through a window. The interior was in disrepair and full of debris, but they saw potential. After learning the property had been foreclosed on by a local bank, they made an offer. But the building they wanted was located on the same lot as the two adjacent buildings—a gas station and warehouse—which were also abandoned. The bank wouldn't split the lot and the price they wanted was beyond what Hamilton and Carli could afford. They walked away.

A year later the properties were still for sale and a representative of the bank contacted them. "Make us an offer," he said. Carli and Hamilton repeated they couldn't afford to buy all three buildings. "Just make us an offer," the man repeated. They offered the same price for all three buildings that they had originally made for the first one alone. This time, the bank accepted. They were now the owners of almost an entire block in the heart of downtown. They couldn't believe their fortune. They were excited. Then they went inside the buildings for the first time.

The buildings came "as-is" and the "is" was much worse than they thought. The amount of rubbish and debris within was colossal. The warehouse contained donated clothes meant for the Katrina hurricane victims that an unscrupulous "philanthropist" had collected and abandoned. Vagrants had gone through the boxes of clothes, dumping each out and robbing the building of anything of value, including the copper wiring. Hamilton admitted he tends to lose heart under such circumstances, but Carli thrives under the challenge. "She is driven," he says. "She'll say, 'if we just do this, then we can do this, which will allow us to do this.' I'll say, 'it will never work,' and she'll say, 'just take the first step.' Which is what we have determined *everything* is. Just small steps."

They dug in. They recruited church groups and volunteers and sorted through *three tons* of clothes that they boxed and shipped to the victims of the Haiti earthquake. They filled and hauled away dumpster after dumpster of junk and trash. The underground water valve serving the property was broken so they dug six feet down into the street through concrete, dirt and rock to replace it. They didn't have the electric power required, so they installed their own utility pole and purchased a transformer from the power company, an $8,000 expense. The floor had caved in, requiring them to bulldoze it and start over. They insulated walls and installed new furnaces. They drained a stagnant pond and built retaining walls and drainage tiles. New water lines, gas lines and bathrooms were installed. Because they needed tenants to help cover expenses an occupancy permit was required, meaning everything had to be brought up to code. And that wasn't easy to do. The occupancy code even specified the distance a door handle must be from the connecting wall. But they did it.

Now the buildings house Hamilton's studio, a potter's studio, the studio of the woodworker Shon Walters, and the headquarters of a theatre company. The Dixons plan to convert another section into a music venue and the abandoned gas station into a drive-through coffee shop. And they did all this in *one year.* They did this while Hamilton continued sculpting and Carli ran her full-time business managing ten full-time employees.

Did I mention they have two children, aged two and five at the time? Carli laughed when I asked her how this was possible. "If someone had written this story six months before it happened, people would have laughed. It seems so unbelievable." They needed furnaces by January for their tenants, and a month before the deadline Hamilton bumped into an acquaintance who happened to have two furnaces worth $2,000 that he didn't need and was willing to sell for $200. The next day someone randomly stopped by the building and offered to pay $200 for unneeded awnings they had removed from one of the buildings. The week they were trying to get rid of the donated clothes, a police officer who was also a minister at a local church stopped by and told them he had a mission going to Haiti and needed donated clothes to take along.

It made a big difference that Hamilton was able to work along with the contractors they hired to keep things on pace and to keep expenses down. When the HVAC man needed a device to hang the heating mechanism that would have cost hundreds of dollars, Hamilton went to his studio and made it. Delay and expense diverted. Carli called vendors and proposed her own payment plans. Most of the time, they accepted immediately. They found a private investor in a time when banks were running scared from properties like theirs.

Metal sculpture by Hamilton Dixon. Photograph by the artist.

Set a vision in motion and serendipitous things happen, they believe. But along with that comes a lot of hard work and the need for a high tolerance for risk. "You have to develop the ability to give up the idea of a safety net," Carli said. They put in long hours and they brought their kids along, including them in the process. Because they both work for themselves, they had the freedom and flexibility to work on the building development between their other projects. (And they didn't need an employer's permission to leave work to meet a contractor.) That's the how, but why? Why endure the headaches, the stress, the hard work, the risks?

"Great cities aren't great because the government sits high in the sky and does wonderful things," Carli said. "Great cities thrive because they have a rich, lively Bohemian street culture that bubbles up and gets people out and moving around."

Okay. But why Dayton? I asked. Carli went to the American University in Washington D.C., where she had as classmates both royalty and the sons and daughters of well-known business tycoons in America. She certainly had opportunities to work in the bustling east coast corporate world. I'll let her explain why:

I loved D.C., but it wasn't my place. When I talk to my friends who still live there, so much of their time and money is spent commuting back and forth, paying ridiculous parking fees, dry cleaning bills, and other lifestyle fees. In the end, it sucks up all their resources just to live the life of being there. Being in Dayton feels like the old West—it's a wide open plain. You want a building downtown? You can get one. Just you. You don't need to be anybody special. You just need to be fearless. I go to an art show, dressed casually with my kids and I'm welcomed and it's genuine. So you are in a place where you see art and true talent. You can expose your kids to almost anything and at the end of the day you can breathe deep and know that you got it all done and feel content that you didn't have too much on your platter. I don't know where else you can do that. It doesn't require a huge volume of money to live in this town. My friends who live in higher priced cities don't have the luxury to think like that.

And because of their vision, fearlessness, and sheer work rate, the city of Dayton has a thriving artists' center that is only going to expand over time. When I met with Hamilton on a cold winter day at his new studio, he was proud of his new space and his accomplishments, even if his body wasn't feeling the best. Years of pounding metal has taken a toll. His right hand was swollen and hurt enough that he questioned his ability to continue forging metal. At the time he couldn't hold a hammer. But his self-doubt was brief.

"Would you ever give it up?" I asked him.

"No," he said. "I'll just learn to hammer with my left hand."

It's that passion that makes a community vibrant. They created a wonderful space, but ultimately Hamilton is a sculptor and will always be. Carli says her biggest accomplishment and reward is being a mother, with her other successes a distant second. They could have used lack of money, family responsibilities, or the risks involved as excuses to avoid taking on what they did. And people wouldn't have blamed them one bit. But they didn't. And my town is the better for it. That's unconventional living.

Places like Greenwich Village, Williamsburg and North Beach weren't thriving artistic communities until people made them so. When Virginia Woolf and Vanessa Bell moved from well-heeled Kensington to Bloomsbury, the latter was considered "respectable but distinctly unfash-ionable," according to biographer Peter Stansky.[xxix] This image was com-pletely changed by Virginia, Vanessa and a handful of others. You can do the same. If you migrate somewhere established, you often arrive too late to take part in its sizzling vibrancy, but early enough to pay the escalated housing costs as the upwardly mobile attracted to the locale's artsy vibe move in and gentrify the neighborhood.

And within your town, consider moving from one section to another in order to reduce your expenses. I bought my home in what many would consider a "distressed" section of town. The same house in a different neighborhood ten miles away would have cost double. But my house payment is modest and I am surrounded by a diverse group of neighbors who are supportive and fascinating. The artists live in my neighborhood; they can't afford the bourgeois McMansions on the outskirts of the city and wouldn't be interested in them if they could.

If you feel unsupported in your community and can't change it, by all means move. But often people move from one place to another because they want to feed off the creativity of others when they are unable to find creativity within themselves. That is escapism and ultimately an illusion. Quentin Carter wrote his best-selling novels while in prison. Emily Dickinson rarely left her house. You can only blame your location so much if you can't draw forth your passion and bliss.

Award-winning novelist Katrina Kittle moved back to Dayton from Brooklyn because she missed the sense of community that Dayton offered, and more. "I have a great tribe of family and friends here, but I mainly came back for the freedom Dayton provides," she told me. "If I stayed in New York, I wouldn't have been able to support myself solely from my writing, which I can do here." The difference in the cost of living allows her to devote her energy to her writing, but she doesn't feel her lifestyle has suffered from being away from New York. She agrees that smaller cities like Dayton have strong cultural and artistic communities if you seek them out. And during her time in Brooklyn, she, like Carli before, discovered that many people living there don't enjoy the cultural offerings available because they are working too much and spending all their money merely to survive. "Dayton is a great jumping off point. Because the cost of living is so reasonable, I can afford to travel to places that I wouldn't otherwise be able to afford," Katrina said.

The humble nature of the smaller cities also allows artistic expression without some of the *attitude* that comes from some of our bigger metropolises. Professional dancer and Bessie Award winner Sheri Williams, who has danced in forty-eight states and on five continents, knows this to be true. "I haven't found a dance company that is as devoid of egos as the Dayton Contemporary Dance Company. If someone has an attitude, it doesn't last long. Some choreographers have reputations as egotists, but when they come here we don't see any of that. That is something they feel they need in places like New York. They don't need it here."

Reevaluate where you live. What does your locale offer that you are not taking advantage of? What does it lack that you can change or build? Living cheaply frees up energy and time to do things that you value. The things you value can probably be found right where you are. If not, create them.

If not you, then who?

The Backdoor Way

I long to let go, drift free of things, to accumulate less, depend on less, to move more simply.

Peter Matthiessen

In many ways, Rick Walkey's and Ali Thomas's lives aren't unusual. They live in a two-story home with their adolescent daughter in a small town. Ali is a performance artist, a dancer, street performer, and is involved with the opera. Rick is a village council member and serves on the local environmental commission and other committees. Their daughter plays on the high school basketball team. Their house feels well lived: bookshelves stacked with books, a bicycle by the door, the upstairs filled with musical instruments. They attest their lives are full, they lack for nothing, and all evidence supports this. What makes their lives unusual is they are able to live this lifestyle on an average combined income of $8,000 a year.[11]

No, that is not a typo. And their ability to live on such a low sum provides them with the wealth that so many of us are denied: *time*. They are rich with time.

Unsurprisingly, most of us define rich differently, and by differently I mean by money. A Gallup poll conducted at the end of 2011 found that the average American believed that to be rich one needed an annual income of $150,000 or more.[xxx] Fifteen percent of those polled believed that an annual income of $1 million or more was needed. Forget being rich—what about just to be *happy?* According to a study by Princeton University in 2011, the average American believes we need $75,000 or more.[xxxi] The average American claims to need almost as much in one *month* as Rick and Ali

---

11 They are not supplementing their income with governmental assistance such as Welfare, Food Stamps, etc.

need in a *year* to have rich and full lives.

How is this possible? Well, their idea of what is a necessity and what provides happiness and wealth is quite different than the average American. "We make enough money to pay for our shelter, our water, our food," Ali said. "Those are real things and it's true, we trade money for that. But people think they need so much more money than they really do." Evidence supports Ali on this. A study done by the University of Michigan found that one year after winning a million dollars or more, lottery winners' happiness drops back down to pre-winning levels.[xxxii]

In our current culture, Rick and Ali's choices seem radical, but it doesn't to them. They are dismayed by people, including some of their friends, who trade big chunks of their lives doing things they would rather do less of, or not at all, for money. Many people observe them wistfully, saying, "I'd like to live like that, but I just can't. I want my kids to go to college." Most of us can appreciate that concern. Rick and Ali don't have a funded retirement account or health insurance, things that most of us aren't willing to go without. But they don't share these fears. "We decided early on, we knew early on, that things were going to be fine, and regardless, money is not security," Ali said. They learned this the hard way. They came into some money and invested it in the stock market right before the 9/11 attacks, and the money disappeared with everyone else's in the crash, as if they never had it. From that point on, they stopped worrying about security and started living their lives day by day with the confidence that they will be able to withstand whatever hurdles life throws at them.

Rick and Ali agree that few people are willing to go the distance they have, and they encourage others to go slowly, trading money and consumption for time gradually, so they can discover where to draw their own lines. They recommend giving up unneeded spending habits before you have to, and once you feel comfortable spending less, let go of the extra work.

When they need or want something, they first ask: how can I make this happen without it costing money? They barter a lot, and trade work for the activities they want in their lives. They enjoy high school sports, so Ali works the ticket booth and they get in free. Ali wanted to go to the opera, so she exchanged acting as an extra in the production for four tickets to each show. She was able to see both the opera and experience the action behind the scenes, while her daughter and husband watched from the seats. They wanted to see the local high school's theater production and instead of spending money on tickets, Ali helped design and sew the costumes for the play. Many of their friends have followed their lead. One, a movie buff, works the popcorn stand at the local theater in exchange for watching the movies.

"People aren't comfortable with this initially, but once you start, everything opens up," Ali said. "Anything you want to do, at all, there's a backdoor way to do it. You don't learn that in school; you just think about money. If you want to eat at a restaurant, talk to the person who owns the restaurant and see what you can do for them. Say: 'I have this skill. Can I trade this skill in order to come eat here once a month?' It can be scary, but take little steps. Don't just quit your job and see how it goes. Whatever you want to do you can find a way to do it without money being involved." Of course taking it to its extreme, bartering can be oppressive, too. If you are working excessively in exchange for stuff or experiences, solely removing money from the equation is not going to lead to happiness. The bartering Rick and Ali advocate is part of the fun itself. It's varied. It's community and neighborhood centered. It's activities and projects they enjoy.

And if they need something and they can't trade, they work for money to pay for it. Ali has a degree in horticulture and Rick is a trained carpenter. They have physical skills that a lot of people don't have (but can have if the choice is made). And they are open and curious. If there is something they haven't done before, they are willing to give it a go. More work is always available if they want it. The difference is, they seldom do. The crucial distinction between them and someone who feels poor is that the amount they earn annually is by choice. They could work more—they turn down work regularly—but their time and freedom is more valuable. This is empowerment, not impoverishment. And often when they do work, it's volunteering, such as organizing a barn-dance fundraiser for the local land trust.

Their story may be exceptional, but it doesn't have to be. And they are not alone. *The Art of Non-Conformity*[xxxiii] author Chris Guillebeau admits he has made as little as $8,000 a year and as much as $250,000 a year. "I can tell you from experience that my happiness level was not significantly different," he writes. I can believe it. As our income rises, our expectations rise as well, but our underlying happiness and contentment seek level ground. We think more is needed, but more is seldom the answer.

As any addict will tell you, over time the pleasure centers of our brains are dulled by our chosen substance and more and more is required to reach the same high. Spending and consumption are no different. What once was a luxury becomes a necessity; when before the midmarket store was a treat, now only the boutique and the brand name will do. It takes a lot to keep up. And we deserve it, we tell ourselves. And maybe we do "deserve" what we really get from this rising need we create in ourselves, and the devil laughs all the way to the bank. At a coffee shop I overheard a first-year student from the local private college whining into her phone about the injustice of her parents buying her a used SUV instead of a new one like most of her friends received. And she *was* genuinely distraught— her feelings were very real. Having such expectations is a recipe for pain. And another middle-aged, very successful couple I know living in Carmel, California were part of a social group that met once a month for a luxurious dinner out in which an alternating couple picked up the bill each time. The cost of each outing ran into the thousands of dollars and when the couple's income dropped during a downturn the strain to remain in the group was immense, but they couldn't fathom dropping out. The shame! The humiliation!

You may not want to reduce your income as much as Rick and Ali have and you probably don't feel the economic pressure of the couple from Carmel, but it is important that you consciously find the balance that works for you. My friends Jamshid and Jennifer have found that balance. Once an engineer for GM, Jamshid quit that job to teach at a local community college at a significant pay cut because he wanted more time to himself and a different work atmosphere. When Jennifer became pregnant, she knew she wanted to be home with their baby. Despite fearing that her employer wouldn't agree (and deciding ahead of time that it was worth losing her job), she asked to reduce her work time to two days a week. To her surprise, her employer agreed. Nothing about their chosen lifestyle is extreme or unusual, but it is thoughtful, consciously chosen, and designed solely based on their values alone. What the Joneses are doing doesn't matter at all. Find your balance. No one will do it for you, and no one should. It is a gift we can only give ourselves.

Fear Is Good If Understood

To conquer fear is the beginning of wisdom.

Bertrand Russell

What prevents most of us from moving forward on our life purpose is seldom lack of ability, inadequate funds, or family responsibility. What holds us back is fear. Fear of making a mistake, fear of losing what we have, and, most importantly, fear we might discover that we lack the capability or talent to achieve our stated goal. It's much easier to nurse the illusion that "if it wasn't for (fill in the blank), I could have been a professional jazz trumpeter." A perfect example of the soul-killing ability of fear is the story of Frank Wheeler in Richard Yates' brilliant novel about 1950s suburban life, *Revolutionary Road.*[xxxiv] Frank and his wife, April, meet and marry in New York City, and move to the suburbs when April becomes pregnant. They rationalize this decision by telling themselves that they are not the stale, soulless people they consider their neighbors to be, but true Bohemians merely biding time while they get on their feet. When April sees through this illusion, she proposes to Frank that he quit his comfortable white-collar job at Knox Business Machines so they can move to Paris, where she will get a job to support them while Frank finds his true calling. Frank agrees, but when it comes time to go, he caves. He can't face the possibility that he may not be an artist, a writer, a musician. He can't face the fear that he may be no different than the suburbanites he enjoys mocking. The Wheelers stay in suburbia and the story ends in tragedy.

Again, I'm not suggesting that one must quit everything and move to Paris to discover oneself. Quite the contrary. But we must analyze what is holding us back, and once we shed our illusions and excuses, we'll find fear hanging around in the shape of a little black demon telling us that we will only fail, so best not try.

Fear is the mind's way of protecting us. It's not fear's job to enhance our lives, to make us grow, or to help us achieve our potential. Fear is there to tell us to run when chased by a lion. Fear is there to keep us from getting so close to the edge of a cliff that we risk falling. Fear helps us avoid doing stupid and destructive things.

But fear can't distinguish between something that is truly dangerous and that which is merely unknown. It tells us to avoid it all. Making this distinction is our job. Fear lets us know that we are pushing past our self-imposed limitations and that we are growing. Fear shows us where our safety zone ends and makes sure we know when we are stepping out of it. When you feel fearful about something, step back and ask yourself: what is it that I am scared of? If you decide that you are scared because the shark's teeth look sharp, it is probably best to stay in the diving cage. That's not cowardice, that's sanity. But if you conclude your decision not to change jobs or reduce your hours is because you are afraid it will lead to failure, push past it. Fear is an adviser, not a dictator.

It's also helpful to ask: what's the worst that could happen? Well, you could fail. And you certainly will from time to time. And we all know failure hurts. Fall in love and you risk a broken heart. Mail off a manuscript and a rejection letter may greet you in the mail. Audition for a part and you may get laughed off the stage. So what. Basil, Zorba's boss, was in love with a widow who lived in the village, but was too afraid to approach her. When Zorba pressures him, Basil says he doesn't want any trouble. Zorba replies, "Life is trouble. Death, no. To live—do you know what that means? To undo your belt and look for trouble." Damn right. This exchange between characters in Salman Rushdie's novel, *The Ground Beneath Her Feet,* sums it up well:

> "I told you not to drink the water if it wasn't boiled."
> "Trouble with you," her smoke blew in my face, "is that you *never* drink the water unless its been boiled for a fucking *year.*"

So you take a risk and the result is not what you wanted. That doesn't mean it's not the best result or the result you need at the time. But if you let fear hold you back you will one day despair over all you have not done. It's better to be Icarus falling from the sky with melted wings than be the schmuck watching him from the ground having never attempted to fly. I challenge you to do this: write down the reasons you use to justify not doing what you really want to do. Then, with precision and honesty bordering on cruelty, cross off the ones that are not truly responsible for your hesitation. Are there any left? If so, what can you do to solve them, even if it takes some time? Put a plan in place, make a timeline, and follow it. If these excuses linger, so will your lack of fulfillment. And remember fear has an upside: facing it can be *exhilarating*. That's why people pay money to skydive or bungee jump despite the intense primal fear of falling that accompanies such acts. And facing what scares you, whether it is starting your own business, having a baby, moving to a foreign country or mailing off a manuscript, will awaken your soul, tantalize your senses and make you feel alive. No matter the outcome. Give yourself that experience. Again. And again. And again.

Love the Stuff You're With (But Own It First)

The Dog and the Shadow

It happened that a dog had found a piece of meat and was carrying it home in his mouth to eat it in peace. Now on his way home he had to cross a plank lying across a running brook. As he crossed, he looked down and saw his own shadow reflected in the water beneath. Thinking it was another dog with another piece of meat, he made up his mind to have that also. So he made a snap at the shadow in the water, but as he opened his mouth the piece of meat fell out, dropped into the water and was lost.

From Aesop's Fables

It sounds so easy, and yet it is so hard. Many of us can't cut back our hours, change jobs, or free up our energy for creative endeavors because we can't stop spending. I've been as guilty as anyone. I love to eat at nice restaurants. When I get an opportunity for exciting travel, I usually take it, even if the expense goes on a credit card. That's been my Achilles' heel. I refuse to live like an ascetic, but I'm getting better at finding balance. I've never been attracted to big toys or expensive cars and I don't live in a McMansion. But when I carry debt, it weighs on me. And that weight consumes life energy that can and should be better spent. Debt, and the possessions and experiences that debt buys, becomes a ball and chain, and there is nothing Bohemian about being a prisoner of our own devices. If we want to begin to move away from the burden of our own comforts, a good place to start is with Aesop's fable about the dog and the wolf.

The Dog and the Wolf

A gaunt wolf was almost dead with hunger when he happened to meet a house-dog who was passing by.

"Ah, cousin," said the dog. "I knew how it would be; your irregular life will soon be the ruin of you. Why do you not work steadily as I do, and get your food regularly given to you?"

"I would have no objection," said the wolf, "if I could only get a place."

"I will easily arrange that for you," said the dog. "Come with me to my master and you shall share my work."

So the wolf and the dog went towards the town together. On the way there the wolf noticed that the hair on a certain part of the dog's neck was very much worn away, so he asked him how that had come about.

"Oh, it is nothing," said the dog. "That is only the place where the collar is put on at night to keep me chained up; it chafes a bit, but one soon gets used to it."

"Is that all?" said the wolf. "Then goodbye to you, Master Dog."

Moral: *better starve free than be a fat slave.*

I have talked of the need to have autonomy in your work, but how many of us are fat slaves to our own bad spending habits? The wolf doesn't have much, but he is free. The dog is well fed, but has no freedom. We chain ourselves to our mortgages, our credit cards, and our need to keep up with the Joneses. Even if you don't spend for status or to compete with others, you may spend money to compensate for deeper longings. In December, 2010, *Newsweek* reported that despite a recent recession and an economy that had still not recovered, American spending had already reached pre-recession levels.[xxxv] One thirty-year-old cocktail waitress interviewed said, "You stop spending and you stop living." I don't share her point of view. But she is not alone. "Entire generations of consumers have grown up with the idea of instant gratification and the credit culture that comes with it," the story reported. I know, it's hard to break free from the temptation to spend; the emotional thrill of buying is real and is ingrained within us and our society. But the thrill is temporary and when the high wears off we feel guilty and often more dissatisfied than before. This behavior is decidedly un-Bohemian and it is time to kick the habit.

Many excellent resources are available to help you curb your spending and get control of your finances but a great place to start is with Adam Baker's website, blog and podcast, *Man Vs. Debt*.[12] At the time he and his wife had their first baby, he was working eighty hours a week and drowning in consumer debt. But the birth of their child triggered them to look at their lives and ask: *What are we doing?* They concluded then and there, sitting at their kitchen table, that they weren't living the lives they wanted and needed to change. Talking it out, they understood they didn't want things; they wanted freedom. They made a plan, sold off all their stuff, paid down $18,000 in consumer debt in a year, and spent the next year traveling through Australia, New Zealand and Thailand. His story and advice are inspiring and practical, and if you are struggling with debt, I highly recommend you check it out.

You won't have the freedom to live the life you want if you are perpetually in debt. You can't have freedom if the amount you spend week in and week out requires you to expend all your mental, emotional and creative energy making money. Very few of us would describe ourselves as materialistic. But we need to walk the talk. Look around you: is your space filled with things you don't need and/or can't afford? Are you surrounded by things you've bought impulsively, things that will wear out quickly and will need to be replaced regularly? Is your space too large, i.e., too expensive for you? In their book, *Your Money or Your Life*,[xxxvi] Joe Dominguez and Vicki Robin advise that we view money as increments of "life energy." When you're tempted to buy something, they encourage you to ask yourself how long and how hard are you going to have to work (i.e., how much life energy you are sacrificing) for the thing you want to buy. Is it worth it? If so, buy it. I am confident when viewed from that perspective, you will find yourself walking out of the store empty-handed more often.

I don't advocate penny-pinching, stinginess, or rigidity of thinking. But wastefulness and excess consumption can become a draining habit.

---

12 manvsdebt.com/

The Abundant Bohemian

When novelist Katrina Kittle visited Ghana, the villages had stores stacked with clean but used soda pop bottles and tin soup cans. The Ghanaians she spoke with didn't understand the concept of Tupperware at all. The food comes in a perfectly good container—why do you need to buy a second one in which to store the food? What silliness! They have a point. As Lily Tomlin joked, we're a culture that goes to the store to buy a trashcan and they put it in a bag, and when we get home we put the bag in the trashcan. As with all choices, approach your spending with awareness and self-knowledge. If you do and you make the choice to spend or buy something, the pleasure you experience will not dissipate the moment you get home.

Another Bohemian characteristic is the ability to distinguish *pleasure* from *diversion*. A pleasure is something that brings you closer to your authentic self; something that provides true joy. A diversion is the exact opposite: something that you do to distract yourself, to pass the time. A pleasure is sustaining; it feeds you. A diversion drains your time, energy and money without enhancing your life at all. This is not a judgment upon any particular activity: one man's pleasure is another's diversion. For me, golf is a diversion; a mild, occasional amusing lark that is ultimately a waste of my valuable time. So I never play it. A friend of mine's Zen-like approach to the game makes it a form of spiritual expression for him. He is as happy playing it alone as with others and he doesn't play for prestige or to enhance business. It provides an authentic experience for him—a true pleasure.

Look at how you spend your time and distinguish between your pleasures and your diversions. Once you have your list, stop engaging in the diversions. Stop wasting your life energy. If you are drawn to a diversion, stop and ask yourself why. What are you avoiding or distracting yourself from? Finishing your painting is hard work, and the only investment you have in the sitcom is the walk to the couch. The sitcom will make you laugh for a brief time. But you know the deeper joy will come when you pick up your brush and go back to the easel. In his research on the sources of happiness, Dr. Jack Bauer, Professor of Social Sciences at the University of Dayton, found that if you are looking to buy happiness, buy experiences instead of stuff. "Experiences like going to a concert or ballgame register more deeply in memory and are often shared with those close to us, which itself breeds happiness. Material goods are often status-oriented, which provides only a brief rush of pleasure and ultimately divides us."xxxvii He further found that "going with the flow" also creates happiness. "Do things that get you focused and in the moment, performing without self-consciousness. Flow takes initial effort, but once you start, flow kicks in. When you're done, you're energized. You've had the experience of being alive. And you're happier." That sounds like being creative. You know what the Bohemian would do, so get going. It's a pleasurable way to live.

Take a moment in your home and close your eyes. When you open them, pretend you are seeing everything for the first time: your furniture, artwork, books, forks and spoons, clothes, everything. Be amazed for a moment in the abundance of all that is present. Pick something up and really look at it. Think about how you have taken the item for granted, have walked past it unconsciously, possibly even buying the same or similar item a second time because you had forgotten what you already owned.

It is okay to have stuff. It is okay to want stuff. But be conscious of it. Be in the present with the material world that you have created. You will find that you need much less, and you will be less tempted to buy more things to crowd your space and to sap your energy. And if you pick something up and you have no attachment to it, get rid of it. Sell it or give it away. Someone else may need it, and you need it out of your space.

Practice the skill of putting things back on the shelf. Before you buy something, leave it alone a few days and if you still want it, go back and get it. You'll find yourself not returning to the store very often. Do you have space in your home or closet for what you are considering buying? There is value in open space, in negative space, in roominess. Don't block the flow of energy in your environment by clogging it up with stuff. A cluttered space results in a cluttered mind.

The Chinese practice of *Feng Shui* is designed to honor the way our environment impacts our lives, and if your space is unorganized, it will be an obstacle. If you respect your space, get rid of what you don't need and

The Abundant Bohemian

honor what you keep, your environment will help you maintain a sense of balance and harmony. This is the atmosphere a true Bohemian needs. Don't squander your resources on accumulation that's going to continue to sap your resources. A Bohemian's bounty comes from within, not without. As you grow to respect this, you won't "suffer" from having fewer possessions than others have or think *you* should have. Understanding this is liberating. Nothing is more bourgeois than having a more-is-better attitude. And ultimately, nothing is more dissatisfying and empty.

Several years ago I visited a friend in Atlanta and together we went to a party thrown by another friend of his, someone I had never met, whom I will call "Tad." Not yet thirty, Tad had amassed quite a bit of wealth, if wealth is defined as the number of possessions owned. To call his home a mansion was not an exaggeration, and the house was stocked with every luxury and toy that an adult could want. Pool, hot tub, boat, jet skis, motorcycle, SUV, sports car. Party room with bar, pool table and large screen television. I've left out a lot. But the man spent the whole day fretting and anguishing over a woman that he was in love with who didn't love him back. Talking with him, observing his mannerisms, his speech, the expression in his eyes and brow, showed he was unhappy and broken-hearted. All his things couldn't give him what he wanted: relinquishment of unrequited love. I had the feeling the party was thrown for the sole purpose of getting this woman to visit when she otherwise would not. I felt like Nick Carraway observing a modern version of Gatsby and Daisy. It was sad to watch.

Not having the stuff wouldn't have made him happy, either. The problem was that he, like all of us have done from time to time, was consuming to fill the emptiness, to create status, and was expecting possessions to solve a problem that possessions can't. You can't mend a broken heart with a jet ski. He would have been better off buying a two dollar notebook and writing a long poem about his pain. He might have found some solace.

Decide what are necessities and buy them guilt-free. When you do buy other things, make sure they will inspire and nourish you. Forget the Hummer. Save your money for paintbrushes and ukulele strings. Place art

81

on your walls, preferably from your painter friend and not a reprint from Target. Have journals and pens handy at all times. Keep the guitar in the corner tuned. Hide the television and put your books on shelves where you can see them. Keep your knitting needles and thread by the sofa. Bring your camera along when you go outside. Use the things you buy to inspire you and keep them nearby so that they are a constant invitation to creation.

Fill your space with color. Use saris as drapes. Fill bowls with fresh fruit. Clear the hallways and closets of junk. Give things away freely. Open the blinds and let the sun in. Make your home a statement of your Bohemian values and not an advertisement that you are a slave to advertisers. And fight the urge for a constant stream of more more more. And the things you do have, love them, care for them, and don't take them for granted. The freedom and lightness you experience will be worth it.

Simplify

The man who has begun to live more seriously within begins to live more simply without.

Ernest Hemingway

I will admit that when I quit my firm and went to work for myself, it took some time to shake off all the "rules" I had absorbed, unchallenged, from my former firm's way of doing things. The need to work, work, work to feed the constant need for more, more, more was what success was all about. Or so I thought.

I came to question this way of life on my own, but I needed help shifting my way of thinking. The attorney with whom I shared office space after I left the firm provided the perfect example of what I wanted to achieve. Tom was in his mid-fifties and married with grown children. He typically showed up at the office around 9:00 a.m., left to meet his buddies for coffee from 10:00 a.m. to 10:30 a.m., and left again for lunch at 11:30 a.m. He would come back and work from 1:00 p.m. to 3:00 p.m. and then went home. He could have worked more hours if he wanted—he wasn't struggling for clients and he wasn't lazy. When hard work was required, he stepped up: earlier in life when a full-time high school teacher and single dad, he commuted ninety minutes in the evenings to attend law school, and still finished in three years.

The hours he works now provide him with adequate income to pay for his needs and wants. He chooses to stop when he has enough and go do other things that fulfill him and give him pleasure. After working with a boss who needed every dime he could squeeze from clients and employees in order to pay for his McMansion and his "successful" lifestyle, Tom's values were a stark contrast.

83

Tom doesn't lack for things; he was able to simplify. He doesn't feel the need to keep up with the Joneses—he drives a reliable but inexpensive car and had a nice, but modest home. He isn't stingy or a penny-pincher. He and his wife travel the world regularly. He just knows the value of things. He knows the value of time. And he knows what he wants, as opposed to what the world tells him he should want. Anne Morrow Lindbergh sums up Tom's philosophy well: "To ask how little, not how much, can I get along with. To say—is it necessary?—when I am tempted to add one more accumulation to my life, when I am pulled toward one more centrifugal activity."

Back to Zorba. Here is Mimiko, the "village idiot," describing his life, after Basil asks him how he spends his days:

> How do you think? I live like a lord! I wake in the morning, I eat a crust. Then I do odd jobs for people, anywhere, anything, I run errands, cart manure, collect horse-dung, and I've got a fishing rod. . . In the evening I go back home, drink a bowl of soup and a drop of wine, if there is any. If there isn't, I drink enough of God's water to make my belly swell like a drum. Then, good night!

He doesn't sound like an idiot to me. The simplicity of his joy rings through. Philosopher and writer Lin Yutang argues that the enjoyment of *leisure* costs less than the enjoyment of *luxury* and is much more rewarding. "All it requires is an artistic temperament which is bent on seeking a perfectly useless afternoon spent in a perfectly useless manner." It doesn't get much more Bohemian than that. Here he goes a bit further:

> No, the enjoyment of an idle life doesn't cost any money. The capacity for true enjoyment of idleness is lost in the moneyed class and can be found only among people who have supreme contempt for wealth. It must come from an inner richness of the soul in a man who loves the simple ways of life and who is somewhat impatient with the business of making money. There is always plenty of life to enjoy for a man who is determined to enjoy it. If men fail to enjoy this earthly existence we have, it is because they do not love life sufficiently and allow it to be turned into a humdrum routine existence.

I don't agree that contempt for wealth is necessary; refusing to over-value it is enough. But he couldn't be more right in saying there is always plenty of life to enjoy. We have this strange need to judge the value of things by their monetary costs. We tend to think that the beach on the other side of the world must be better than the one close by because it costs a lot more and takes a long time to get there. While I was in law school, the Dean told me an interesting story. If the number or quality of the applicants to the school fell, they raised the tuition and the numbers came back up. Not because of an increase in programs, test scores, or job placement—the school remained the same. More people applied because they assumed more expensive meant better. That's all there was to it. This sounds crazy, and it is. But it is a habitual way of thinking that we are all guilty of from time to time. You are probably wasting money somewhere because you think spending the money will somehow make things better. Become aware of this and curb your habit.

Try taking a spending fast. Pick one week, or if you're brave, a month, and limit your spending to one-fourth, one-third, or even one-half of what you normally spend. Be disciplined. After the time is up, reflect upon your experience. Did you miss the spending that much? Do you feel freer, more in control, or suppressed and unrewarded? It may be more difficult than you expect at first, but I bet you will discover your happiness was not wrapped up with the spending and consuming as much as you thought. If true, you have gained a new power over your life. If not, at least you have a better understanding of the experience of those who have less, will have more compassion and will take a greater joy in your abundance.

Picasso once said that art is the elimination of the unnecessary. Make your life your art. Eliminate the unnecessary, the superfluous, the shackles and the crutches. Your spending will decrease and your need to sacrifice your life energy to make money will decrease, giving you more time to be Bohemian. Both Mimiko, the village idiot, and Lin Yutang, the professor-philosopher, will be proud of you.

Forget Retirement

Enjoy yourself, it's later than you think.
Enjoy yourself, while you're still in the pink.
You work and work for years and years, you're always on the go.
You never take a minute off, too busy making dough.
Someday, you say, you'll have your fun when you're a millionaire.
Imagine all the fun you'll have in some old rocking-chair.

"Enjoy Yourself" music by Carl Sigman and lyrics by Herb Magidson

You can't swing a dead cat without hitting somebody with an anecdote about someone they knew who worked forty years at the same place and died six months after retiring, usually while planning his around-the-world adventure. Stories like this always carry a feeling of regret because the protagonist is usually the type that was going to start "living" in retirement, because, as everyone knows, that's when the good life starts. It's never a wise choice to live an unsatisfied life believing that you will make up for it later, but I'll discuss that momentarily.

I'm going to challenge you with the notion that you should give up the idea of retiring altogether; that "retirement" is an anti-Bohemian concept. Working too hard now, sacrificing too much now, so that you don't have to work at all later is self-defeating. It's like starving for a week and then gorging yourself on an eight-course meal when you're too hungry to even taste the food. It's not healthy and the pleasure deferred is pleasure lost forever.

Several years ago I invited a friend to join me on a European trip, but he declined because he didn't want to travel until he had funded his 401(k) plan to a certain level. I ended up traveling with other friends. A few years later, the money he had not spent on the travel was lost when the stock market crashed, but I still have the memories and experiences.

Am I advising not to plan ahead or save for a rainy day? Of course not. But find balance. Be both the ant and the grasshopper: live now and plan ahead. Put money away, by all means, but give up your cable television and designer purses, not your art supplies or travel budget. Based on the current state of the Social Security program in the United States (expected to run out by 2033) and the average American's savings, retirement may be an option few of us will have. The answer is to continue to work in the Bohemian way, which is the same way you should strive to work all your life: enough to satisfy your needs without depriving you of the time and energy for creative expression.

If for no other reason, do it for your health. A study published by the *British Medical Journal* in 2005 found that those who retire at age fifty-five have a significantly increased risk of early death as compared with those who retire at sixty-five.[xxxviii] Recently University of Zurich economist Josef Zweimüller conducted a similar study that found for every extra year of early retirement, a worker loses two months of life expectancy.[xxxviii] The anecdotes are true: without a sense of purpose people atrophy both mentally and physically. Dayton-based author Fred Arment encourages people to view this stage of life not as retirement, but as "reinspirement." After selling his successful marketing and advertising business at age forty-seven, he "retired." But instead of choosing to wind down his days on the golf course or in front of the television, he has used this period of time to write two novels, one nonfiction book (he writes no less than two hours a day six days a week), and help create the first International Peace Museum and the International Cities of Peace program, a program that in only three years has thirty-three committed cities from all over the world. He also found time to spend seven winters living on his sailboat and touring the Caribbean. In his experience, the majority of his friends have been excited about retirement, but once it's reached, they became terrified. Each moment is a decision, and we all need purpose, regardless of age. "You have to get re-inspired, or you'll die," he said. "Like a shark in water, you have to keep moving, to keep breathing to keep alive. In my experience only about half of retirees are able to do this."

Author and English professor Ed Davis struggled with these issues when he faced retirement after thirty-five years of teaching. Teaching was his calling, and he felt good about what he did and the contribution he made to his students' lives. But he still had bad days, and on those days retirement looked good. But as the big day approached, he began to wonder—who will he be if not a teacher? In his fantasy, he would have all this time to write, to produce great works. Writing fiction requires a lot of time, and teaching was consuming much of his. When it came to his writing, he was always "getting to it." "I wanted to get there; to have that freedom. And retirement was going to be the great salvation."

Initially, rather than being his salvation, retirement was his curse. Not going to the college each day made him feel he lacked structure (the very thing he loathed throughout most of his career) and purpose. "I'm not as important to young people in the way I once was," he said. "You miss being important. A sense of power loss lets age creep in. The loss of status was surprisingly hard to accept." He was plagued by the question: "I got here, and now what do I do?" Paradoxically, this extra time and lack of work responsibility inhibited his writing instead of freeing it. He didn't want to write one more unpublishable novel. And yet, writing was what he always wanted to do; it's what he's always done. He felt isolated and suffered from depression. A psychiatrist prescribed antidepressant medications and he carried the prescriptions around in his wallet for a year, but never had them filled. Instead, he slowly began writing again. And getting back to what he loved, re-engaging his passion and changing his attitude from *retirement* to Arment's *reinspirement* was exactly what he needed. He used both fiction and nonfiction to work through his feelings and experiences, and this helped him move through the depression. "Writing to me is a magical, mystical, sacred thing. Just showing up at the writing table, is what saved me." Ed's retired in the sense that he doesn't go to the college and draw a paycheck any more. But he writes. He teaches workshops and runs writing salons. He coaches and supports other writers. He is engaged with the world around him, producing and contributing *good things*, and when you do that, it's hard to stay depressed.

Author Mark Nepo's life-threatening disease caused him to reevaluate his belief in deferring enjoyment of the present in order to protect from future, possible dangers. Having survived his brush with death, he sees things differently. "Now, on the other side, my mind has been reformed and deferring anything that might ignite joy, that might help loved ones grow *now,* deferring *anything real,* seems dangerous," he wrote.

Being nowhere near retirement myself, Nepo's, Arment's and Davis's experiences teach me the value of seeking freedom from unwanted burdens while striving to remain engaged and energized by meaningful work. I will no longer rely on an idea of a future event or life-change to bring me joy. There is no golden ticket at the end that isn't already in our pockets. We must be engaged in life now and be engaged later. We can't delay happiness—all we have is the present. You want to retire so you can travel? Travel now. You want to retire so you can paint? Paint now. Give up the excuses and the half-baked dreams of the future used to justify putting things off. The experiences you will have at sixty-five will be just as valuable, but will not be the same ones you would have had at twenty, thirty, or fifty. Don't sacrifice them at the altar of delayed joy. Make money now, somehow; do what fulfills you now, somehow, and just keep going. What is unconventional about such a life is the unbelievable fact that so few people are willing to do it. The present is all we have, and in the present is where the Bohemian needs to live.

It's Great to Be Anywhere

It's great to be here. It's great to be anywhere.

Keith Richards

You could be dead by evening.

Proust

Like those who put off life until retirement—that magical future day when they can start "living"—each of us makes the same mistake on smaller levels every day. Always reliving the past or fretting over the future, we miss the value of the present. I was receiving a massage when I realized how hard it was for me to stay in the moment. I was sore and stressed out and had looked forward to my appointment all week. When the time came, it was great—for a little while, before my thoughts took over. Slowly, I began fretting over how much time had passed since the massage began and how much time I had left before it would end. Then I became lost in thoughts about that afternoon and work tomorrow and what I should have said to that rude salesclerk earlier. When I realized what I was doing I became annoyed at my ridiculousness. I couldn't enjoy my massage— something peaceful, pleasant and relaxing—because I couldn't be *present*. How was I to find peace in the less pleasant times, the hectic times? This felt like insanity, and according to Abraham Maslow, it is. "The ability to be in the present moment is a major component of mental wellness," he wrote. I wasn't living in the present, which means, ultimately, that I wasn't really living. This was an epiphany to me, and one that I work at—success is difficult to maintain—every day. There are many ways to practice being present and many resources to draw from. Because the ability to stay present is so important, I'm going to touch on a few key concepts and hope that you choose to explore them further.

Hemingway once wrote, "I have stood on the crowded back platform of a seven o'clock bus as it lurched along the wet, lamp-lit street while men who were going home to supper never looked up from their newspapers as we passed Notre Dame, gray and dripping in the rain." He wrote this when young and living in the poor section of the Latin Quarter in Paris. While the people around him were wrapped up in the daily transitory news, Hemingway was experiencing the joy of the present moment by viewing the beauty of one of the world's most sacred places as it was washed by rain.

Anaïs Nin experienced similar joys by staying present and observing the world. Describing one morning, she wrote, "A leaf fluttered in through the window this morning, as if supported by the rays of the sun, a bird settled on the fire escape, joy in the task of coffee, joy accompanied me as I walked." To be an artist, you must cultivate this presence. "To be an artist was to see what others could not," said Patti Smith. I learned to experience what Patti describes from taking a drawing class. Afterward I observed the world differently; I paid closer attention to colors, lighting and shadows. My conscious observing allowed me to see the world with heightened intensity. If you are not present, you risk missing the beauty each moment potentially brings, even during mundane activities.

N.C. Wyeth's children said that when N.C. drove them home on moonlit nights he often stopped, turned off his headlights, and said to them, "Isn't this gorgeous?"[xxxix] Doing so instilled in them the importance of living in the moment and appreciating beauty that is both free and abundant. Try this yourself the next time you are in a public place and hear someone braying inanity into a cell phone. Pause and soak up everything that he is missing: the feel of the breeze, the sound of the birds singing and of feet shuffling on the sidewalk, the vision of a woman reading on a park bench. You will feel more at ease, more grounded and more content. Practice this.

Live more deliberately, intentionally and purposefully, spiritual coach Duane Elgin advises. But how? Stop seeking distraction. Few of us can wait five minutes at a bus stop without checking for or sending text messages. Resist this. Writer Brenda Ueland recommends asking yourself questions about the moment to pull you back into it:

Sometimes say softly to yourself: *"Now* . . . now. What is happening to me now? This is *now.* What is coming into me now? This moment?" Then suddenly you begin to see the world as you had not seen it before, to hear people's voices and not only what they are saying but what they are trying to say and you sense the whole truth about them. And you sense existence . . . as a translucent whole.

Rumi advises to "sell your cleverness and buy bewilderment." Exercise your senses like you would your muscles. Watch how a child will bend over and really *look* at a frog, or a flower. Emulate that. Stare at a dragonfly as if you've never seen one before and experience the bewilderment that is unavoidable. Here is Basil describing Zorba's love of what is real and present:

"What is that mystery?" he asks. "What is a woman, and why does she turn our heads? Just tell me, I ask you, what's the meaning of that?" He interrogates himself with the same amazement when he sees a man, a tree in blossom, a glass of cold water. Zorba sees everything every day as if for the first time.

And here are the words of the man himself:

"I've stopped thinking all the time of what happened yesterday. And stopped asking myself what's going to happen tomorrow. What's happening today, this minute, that's what I care about. I say: 'What are you doing at this moment, Zorba?' 'I'm sleeping.' 'Well, sleep well.' 'What are you doing at this moment, Zorba?' 'I'm working.' 'Well, work well.' 'What are you doing at the moment, Zorba?' 'I'm kissing a woman.' 'Well, kiss her well, Zorba! And forget all the rest while you are doing it; there's nothing else on earth, only you and her! Get on with it!'"

Spoken like a Zen master. Are you working a job that is less than satisfactory? Change it. If you can't change it presently, then really engage it, do it the best you can and take joy in it. Fantasizing about something else you could be doing is unproductive and life-wasting. If you are washing the dishes, then really wash the dishes. Don't dwell on yesterday or tomorrow. This moment is all you have, again and again and again until there are no more moments. Scary, yes, but also freeing. You need to be present in order to free your spirit and allow the Bohemian in you full expression. "When I walk in a carefree way, without straining to get to my destination, then I am living *in the present*. And it is only then that the creative power flourishes," Brenda Ueland wrote.

Being present makes you creative, happy and sane. "I've lived out my melancholy youth," wrote Henry Miller. "I don't give a fuck anymore what's behind me, or what's ahead of me. I'm healthy. Incurably healthy. No sorrows, no regrets. No past, no future. The present is enough for me. Day by day. Today! *Le bel aujourd'hui!*" Damn right. How sad that so many can't claim to live that life. But not you. Right now you are reading this book, not worrying about the project due on Monday or fretting over the insult your sister gave you a week ago. And if you are? Note it, forgive yourself, and come back. The present is where the "awe" can be found. Petty things fall away, you see the beauty in all that is around you, and those moments make it all worthwhile. This poignant passage from the film *A Single Man* sums it up nicely:

A few times in my life I have had moments of absolute clarity. When for a few brief seconds the silence drowns out the noise and I can feel rather than think and things seem so sharp and the world seems so fresh. It is as if it had all just come into existence. I can never make these moments last. I cling to them but like everything they fade. I've lived my life on these moments. They pull me back to the present. And I realize everything is exactly the way it's meant to be.[xi]

Because it will end, my friend. For you, for me, for everyone we know. Breathe in the glory of our mortality and the gifts we are given between birth and death. Life is worthy of it. Living in blindness, dullness, and unconsciousness is a choice we cannot make. That's choosing not to choose. When we drift away, we must pull ourselves back to the Now.

The Fable of the Shepherd

A shepherd lived long ago, and in his culture it was expected that one sacrifice an animal to God each year at harvest. The shepherd was poor and had only two sheep, and he and his family loved them very much. When it came time to sacrifice one of them, he couldn't bring himself to

93

do it. God came to him and demanded the sacrifice. But the shepherd's love for his animals was so great that he asked if he could sacrifice himself in their place.

"You would rather give your life in exchange for the lives of these creatures?" God replied. The shepherd looked at his sheep, saw their pleading eyes, and said yes.

"Then I accept your offering," said God.

But when the shepherd looked to his wife and small children standing in the doorway, he grew worried for them. "Will you grant me one request?" he said to God. "May I live long enough to raise my sons into men so that they may take care of themselves and my wife after I am gone? For they would surely suffer and die without my care."

"Because your sacrifice is great, I will grant your wish. You shall have twenty years and then I will come for you." God left and the shepherd was much relieved.

The shepherd awoke the next morning and as he did every day, he went to his window to watch the sunrise. But this morning he felt different. "I only have twenty years of sunrises left to savor," he thought. And this thought heightened his joy and appreciation. And at the end of the day, he stopped and reflected back on the work he had done, the time he had spent with his family, and the moments of solitude he had found, and every part of his day held great joy. Knowing that his time in this place was limited allowed him to be present and to love everything in a way that he had not known before.

When fall came, he thought, "I have only nineteen falls left." But instead of bringing him sorrow, this knowledge allowed him to revel in the changing colors and he often sat under his tree and stared for hours at a single leaf. When the long winter came and his wife complained about the cold and the snow, he would pull her close and say, "Don't rush the season along. Look at how beautiful the earth sleeps. Come and sit by the fire." Every meal was savored. "How many more luscious strawberries shall I have?" he asked himself. He knew they were numbered.

And when each child's birthday came, he celebrated with great joy. His family didn't understand the change in him, but his love and joy was contagious and they became happier and more appreciative too. Every morning the man woke and said, "I have four thousand sixty-three days left," or "I have twelve winter solstices left," and he took pause to bask in the glow of everything he had and loved. And in this way his twenty years passed. In that time his sons grew to be strong men and his wife was content.

On his last day, he rose like any other. He kissed his wife and took his flock to the fields to graze before his sons awoke. God met him in the fields.

"Are you ready?" God said.

The shepherd smiled and nodded.

"Do you regret your choice?" God asked.

"No," he responded. He waved his hand across the hundreds of sheep that made up his flock and said, "These are all children of the sheep I spared the day you demanded a sacrifice. Their offspring have spread and will feed and provide for my family for many years to come. And each day I have lived has been a gift so much more precious by my knowing that each was one of a very limited number. I have lived lifetimes in my twenty years. I have had many friends and foes who have died these last twenty years having lived their life asleep, putting off their joy until tomorrow and fretting over petty things. Many died with anger and resentment in their hearts. They knew not what life was worth. I have lived well, I am ready, and I thank you for what you have given me."[13]

My mother was a Get-On-With-It person. This was an attribute professionally—she was successful and accomplished much. And when she came home from work she wasn't one to lounge around. Her house was always clean and she had a beautiful garden. When she was being still I could watch her face (her lips often moved when she silently talked to herself) working out something that needed to be done, a habit I inherited from her. She rarely took time off and when she did, it was for family events, such as planning big get-togethers for the holidays or traveling to one of my or my brother's many soccer tournaments.

In 2004, at the age of fifty-eight, she was diagnosed with stomach cancer. Despite having chemotherapy and even having her stomach removed (yes, you can live without a stomach—the intestine adapts) the cancer had spread throughout her body. In January of 2005, I took her and my father to Puerto Vallarta, Mexico. She had previously never been out of the country. Wheelchair bound, she reveled in bouncing along the bumpy, cobblestone streets, taking in the bright colors of the painted buildings, fabrics and glassware. She loved bartering with the merchants and ordering exotic and beautiful food she knew she would not be able to eat. Sitting on the beach, she watched the ocean for hours.

On the day before we left I pushed her wheelchair out to the sand and we sat and watched the sun set over the ocean. We were quiet for a long stretch of time before she spoke.

"It's so great to be here, isn't it?" she said.

"Yes," I said. "I love Mexico."

"Yes, but I mean it's so great to be *here*."

And then I knew what she meant. It was great to be here, alive, now, in the present moment. And I could feel the bittersweet realization she had come to, and I witnessed the sense of peace, not regret, that it gave her.

---

13 This fable was inspired by Joe Durzo.

We returned home and a month later she died. Despite the horrible physical suffering she endured (and cancer is *god-awful*—no one should experience what my mother experienced), that sense of peace and presence never left her. When she passed away, she was ready.

When I get wrapped up with my to-do list and am biting my lip and talking to myself anxiously over this or that, in my best moments I catch myself and go back to the beach, sitting on the sand next to my mother, and remind myself how great it is to be *Here.* I slow down, I pay attention, and I look at things as if seeing them for the first time. I try to look at things as if seeing them for the last time. I remind myself to be bewildered and experience rapture, one moment at a time. My problems shrink to their proper, insignificant size, and I am again at peace. Thanks, Mom.

Slow Down

Everybody seems to think I'm lazy
I don't mind, I think they're crazy
Running everywhere at such a speed
Till they find, there's no need

"I'm Only Sleeping," by John Lennon & Paul McCartney

Nothing is more vulgar than haste.

Ralph Waldo Emerson

Describing the management at his company, a client said, "We never have time to do it right, but always have time to do it over again." I could relate, as this was how I once worked. In order to get the most done, to multitask and maximize output, I tried to do many things at once and rush through them all. Needless to say, I ended up having to redo or correct much of what I had done due to my lack of focus and patience, and the correcting usually took twice as long as the time it would have taken to do it right in the first place. I wasn't multitasking; I was half-tasking several things at once.

"Hurry, hurry brings no blessing," advises a Swahili proverb, and that is a hard lesson to learn in our culture. And once learned, we easily slip back into old habits. When I slip, I have plenty of time to reflect on my regret as I'm repeating the task for a second time. The pressure in our culture to do-more-faster carries over into our personal lives as well. Most people today equate leisure and fun solely with activity. The idea of being still, to lie under a shady tree and stare at the clouds is not only boring but *a waste of time*. They could be using that time productively by going to amusement parks or playing video games. They get anxious when still, quiet, or alone.

Dylan Thomas grew to dislike America due to what he described as its "barbaric speed." He has a point.

This problem is not new, and America does not suffer from it alone. "And so, when the entertainment which busy people find even in business is withdrawn, their mind cannot endure home, loneliness, walls and cannot abide itself left to itself," Seneca wrote two thousand years ago. In *Romantic Rebels*, Emily Hahn wrote that Bohemian Henry Clapp found the rapid speed of American life difficult after being abroad. Describing his return to New York in 1850 after an extended stay in Paris, she wrote, "The New York cafés did not please him. The clientele had the awful American restlessness, gulping down their beer and rushing away before any discussion could even start, much less finish." This condition is in our blood. "Most men pursue pleasure with such breathless haste that they hurry past it," said Søren Kierkegaard.

I know many people who turn the television on the moment they walk in the door, claiming it keeps them company, or offers white noise. I'm guilty of wanting to reach for my iPod or a book when I'm alone. But is occupying all our moments with activities and distractions what we want, or have we just lost the skills to stop the busyness? I believe the latter. When she placed herself in the cultures of Italy, India, and Bali, Elizabeth Gilbert, as she wrote in *Eat, Pray, Love*, concluded that "Americans don't really know how to do *nothing*."[xli] Lin Yutang thinks we want to be able to do nothing, but can't or won't give ourselves the permission to be still. "I am quite sure that amidst the hustle and bustle of American life, there is a great deal of wistfulness, of the divine desire to lie on a plot of grass under tall beautiful trees of an idle afternoon and *just do nothing*," he wrote.

This wistfulness for a slower life is as present in America today as when Yutang wrote those words seventy years ago. He romanticizes this idea through the image of the vagabond, a romantic hero representing something we feel we have lost in our modern world. Franco-Czech novelist Milan Kundera agrees. He writes:

Why has the pleasure of slowness disappeared? Ah, where have they gone, the amblers of yesteryear? Where have they gone, those loafing heroes of folk song, those vagabonds who roam

The Abundant Bohemian

from one mill to the other and bed down under the stars?[xlii]

I'd like to apply for that job position: one who travels from town to town, telling stories and playing songs for his dinner and sleeping under the stars. Today such a person is called homeless, and is lucky if he is merely arrested as opposed to being molested or attacked for his trouble. (Although I suppose the definition could apply to modern day indie musicians.) There was a time when it was believed that technology would save us; that machines would do our labor and we wouldn't need to spend the majority of our day working. Lin Yutang again:

> After all, the machine culture is rapidly bringing us nearer to the age of leisure, and man will be compelled to play more and work less . . . The constant rush for progress must certainly one day reach a point when man will be pretty tired of it all, and will begin to take stock of his conquests in the material world . . . no one can predict anything about the next century.

Yutang wrote that in the 1930s, and reading it makes me wistful for what-might-have-been because we know how things turned out. But it's not too late, at least for the Bohemians out there. We must first learn to honor and respect the act of doing nothing. One must ask: am I free, or am I an indentured servant to my busyness, habits, and distractions? If you don't like the answer your soul gives you, it's time to slow down. The push to do-more-faster is now facing organized resistance. In Milan in 2007 the first International Day of Slowness was observed. This day was created, as reported in *Newsweek* by Malcolm Jones, for the purpose of celebrating, "Stepping out of the fast lane by doing less, taking your time at it, and reflecting more on it."[xliii] The Slow Food movement was formed (also in Italy) as a ballast against the fast food culture and promotes the meal as the languid, sensual, pleasurable, cultural event it is. The Slow Food movement has since spawned the Slow Travel movement, the Slow Money movement, and the Slow Reading movement. The names speak for themselves, and promote the desire to have richer, deeper experiences with our pleasures instead of gulping them down and racing through them with breakneck speed. [14]

"The essence of pleasure is spontaneity," wrote Germaine Greer. She's right, but unless we make the conscious choice to slow down, spontaneity is a gift we deny ourselves. Try this test: decide to do something on the spur of the moment and ask a friend to join you. There is a high probability the conversation will go something like this:

"Would you like to [fill in the blank] with me?"

"When?"

"Now."

"What? Now? I can't go now. I have to take Ashley to ballet and then coach Nick in soccer tonight."

"How about tomorrow?"

"I can't tomorrow. I'm meeting Bill at Home Depot to pick out a new ceiling fan. The day after that would have been possible, but Bill has his softball league and it's too late to get a babysitter. You should have called earlier. I'm available a week from Sunday though. How about that?"

By this point, you've probably lost interest in doing anything at all. I'm not devaluing children's activities or home improvement projects. And many of my childless friends are just as busily scheduled. But when do people have time to be spontaneous? Do we need to schedule time on our calendar for it? "A week from Thursday I've set aside two hours to be spontaneous!" It doesn't work that way. In Louis Begley's novel, *About Schmidt*,[xliv] Schmidt has a conversation with his daughter in which she tells him how busy and involved her child is. He asks her: when does the child have time for an inner life? I wonder the same thing about many of the children I see growing up in my community today. These children become adults and they don't know how to be still, they don't know how to be alone, and they don't know how to be spontaneous. This constant scheduling and over-emphasis on activities has negative consequences on our children's health, too, causing anxiety, fatigue and attention deficit problems.[xlv] Fellow Bohemians, this is not acceptable. Set an example and let others follow.

---

14 For a fun reminder to slow down, go to http://www.adbusters.org/abtv/slow_down_week.html and watch the one-minute cartoon supporting National Slow Down Week.

Don't live every moment of every day by your e-calendar. Exchange rigidity and constant structure for flexibility and lighthearted ease. Listen to the wind from time to time and go where it takes you. To do this, you must learn the art and the pleasure of slowing down. Slowing down allows us to pay attention to that which is around us. Slowing down allows us to see possibilities that we would otherwise miss in our frantic pursuit of what we think we want. Slowing down allows us to experience life in a deeper and richer way, whether when eating our food, walking through fall leaves, or listening to a lover tell of her day. Scottish poet Kathleen Jamie described writing poetry as the "Art of listening. Listening with attention. Bringing the quality of attention to the world." I say reading poetry requires the same attention; attention most of us don't want to give. Author Carl Honoré realized his need to slow down when he found himself hurrying through his nightly ritual of reading to his son, going as far as skipping pages and scenes altogether.[xlvi] We all fall prey to such acts and because of that, we miss out on much.

So how do we slow down in our frantic, media-blitzed culture? It's not easy, but a few simple rituals that you can add to your day can make a tremendous difference. Try waking up fifteen minutes earlier than you have to and use this time to be quiet, alone and reflective. This prevents the day from feeling rushed and busy from the minute the alarm goes off and you jump out of bed. Don't check your email, social media or read the paper in that fifteen minutes, but rather meditate, go for a walk outside, or just sit on your front steps and breathe in the morning. Use a few minutes of this morning time to write in a gratitude journal, noting what you are thankful for from the previous day and what you'd like to experience in the day ahead of you.

During the day take technology breaks by refraining from going on-line or checking your phone for at least an hour at a time. Step outside your workplace and go for a slow meandering stroll for fifteen minutes. At the end of the day, focus on what you accomplished instead of the tasks you didn't get done. Making these simple steps a habit will reward you. Bringing slowness into the day has proven health benefits, reducing anxiety, stress, depression and the accompanying physical ailments that result. We are all busy and have many responsibilities, but it is a mistake to think you don't have the time—or the right—to carve out this space for yourself. You'll be more successful and fulfilled with your family and work if you do, and that's good for everybody.

But there will always be days in our lives where the hectic strain of life overpowers us. Sometimes my thinking becomes so speedy that I need to slow it down by stopping, cold turkey, from engaging with social life altogether. At that point I crave quiet and aloneness like water or exercise. I crave the gift of solitude.

Solitude and Nature

Now, instead of planting our solitude with our own dream blossoms, we choke the space with continuous music, chatter and companionship to which we do not even listen. It is simply there to fill the vacuum. When the noise stops there is no inner music to take its place. We must re-learn to be alone.

Anne Morrow Lindbergh

Add to Ms. Lindbergh's list emailing, texting, tweeting, Facebook posting, and Xbox playing. I wonder what she would think about the value we put on solitude today. Many of us can't spend *any* time in solitude—the questions the silence allows to surface cause too much anxiety. But those moments when we are free of distraction challenge us to look within and acknowledge what we are really feeling. Sadly, we often realize we don't like our lives all that much. It's time to change that and that means spending some time alone.

Look at how the majority of people are living their lives and you will see that the choice to spend time alone is choosing to live unconventionally. And when I say alone, I don't mean a Sunday afternoon watching television by yourself—I mean choosing *solitude*: the act of removing yourself from escapist stimulation in order to allow reflection. Be still and present and see what is drawn from within instead of absorbing the projections of others. You'll be amazed at what you discover. View it as an internal re-grouping. By pulling oneself together we once again reacquaint ourselves with our true nature. Again, Anne Morrow Lindbergh:

When one is a stranger to oneself then one is estranged from others, too. If one is out of touch with oneself, then one cannot touch others . . . Only when one is connected to one's own core is one connected to others . . . and that can best be refound through solitude.

There is no better way to slow down and experience solitude than to spend time in nature. I wrote this following the morning of the first of May when I enjoyed a slow, leisurely breakfast followed by a walk in the woods. A warm drizzling rain fell intermittently, exposing a lushness to the foliage that felt tropical. The rain didn't deter the birds from singing and I glimpsed the wings of a heron taking flight above the slow-moving river that ran along the trail. I moved at an easy pace and stopped to view the most rotund sycamore I had ever observed in my home state of Ohio, one as majestic as the sequoias I had marveled at in California. Some trees in the reserve were alive before Columbus landed.

The morning flew by in the way time does when one is enjoying oneself, but, paradoxically, the day felt slow, languid and full. "No man should go through life without once experiencing healthy, even bored solitude in the wilderness," Jack Kerouac said. I wasn't bored that day, but I know what he means. We need consciously to step away from the clutter of the material world and let the domestic, both trivial and serious, fall away for a time. While in the forest, I do not feel anxious, hurried, annoyed or concerned I should be doing something else. My worries will be waiting for me when I return to society, but something in our DNA allows us to leave our stresses in the car when we enter the natural world. And we suffer when we ignore this need. Joseph Campbell believed we must create time to spend in nature, even if it's just to take a walk in the country over the weekend. "But if in your weekend or holiday you keep yourself in the world of enclosed civilized living, the nature inside you becomes starved," he wrote. When artist Diego Rivera was creatively blocked, he took solace in nature. "More soothing [than hanging around the cafés] were long walks, excursions through the various quarters of Madrid and the Castilian countryside, talks with workingmen and peasant folk," wrote his biographer and friend, Bertram Wolfe. "When with them, he listened much and talked little, observed, sketched, thought. The sketches were more truly Rivera than the formal paintings into which they later dissolved." By taking time in nature your senses will awaken and the fullness of life will become impossible to ignore. Visualize yourself following 17th century Chinese philosopher

The Abundant Bohemian

Chang Ch'ao's advice:

> One should listen to the sounds of birds in spring, to the sounds of cicadas in summer, to the sounds of insects in autumn and the sounds of snowfall in the winter; he should listen to the sounds of pine trees in the mountains, and the sounds of ripples on the waterside. Then he shall not have lived in vain.

Isn't it soothing to merely envision oneself listening in that way? I close my eyes and think of the sound of snowfall and I can feel my blood pressure drop. *The sound of ripples on the waterside.* Paying attention to these sounds is an act of meditation in itself.Communion with water has been the choice for many of us who need a respite from the frantic mainstream. The next time you are near an ocean, lake or river, skip the speedboat and Sea-Doo and find something that you can lie in and bob along with the current. How much do you care about the insult your boss gave you when you are being rocked on a sleepy river, listening to the slap of the water against the hull, or resting at the shore listening to the sound of the ripples with Chang Ch'ao?

But you don't need to travel to the country or the ocean to experience the solitude that nature offers. Richard Powell, author of *Wabi Sabi Simple*,[xlvii] was able to experience this by "taking time after supper in the summers to sit quietly in the living room, let the sunlight fade off the trees, let the gray twilight usher in the little brown bats while watching serenely the stars come out one at a time in the darkening sky. Let the night happen." Notice he doesn't talk of making things happen, but *letting* them happen. Let go. Be part of it. Nature offers these gifts freely, we only need observe and experience. Cable television can't compare, and that costs money. Turn it off, step outside, listen and breathe. After reading Powell, I try to make an evening walk through my yard and garden a daily ritual. Even in spaces as limited as an urban backyard, the constant growth and change is expansive and grounding. One flower closes only for another to bloom. I may have another tomato, blackberry, or cucumber ready to be picked. Any given day I'll see butterflies, moths, bees, fireflies, hummingbirds, squirrels, rabbits, and dozens of species of birds. Ah, city life!

"To sit alone on a quiet night—to invite the moon and tell her one's sorrow—to keep alone on a good night—and to call to the insects and tell them one's regret," Chang Ch'ao wrote on an evening well spent. One regret I have to tell the insects is that I don't speak to them more often. One evening my companion and I made a fire in our backyard and sat together for several hours talking, but not really. Mainly we were quiet and still, watching the fire and the dusk fall and listening to the birds' decreasing song. We went to bed unusually content without needing to contemplate why. When one allows oneself to just *be*—as foreign an act as it has become for most of us, the "why" ceases to be relevant.

Each part of the day offers its own beauty. At night, when the birds have quieted, the dogs have stopped barking and the world readies for sleep, if one gives oneself up to the vastness of the sky, it is impossible not to become consumed by awe. Peter Matthiessen received this advice from his Zen Master, Soen-roshi: "Swallow the stars until you are one with the universe, with all-pervading universal life!" That's the feeling one gets when quiet and alone in the deep of night; it is impossible not to reflect on bigger things. The stillness slows our biorhythms and even as you get sleepy, you experience clarity that is difficult to find in the bustle of the day. It is a beautiful feeling, and it is sad that so many of us don't experience it more often. But as you wake and nurture the Bohemian inside of you, I promise you will. You will see things—truly see them—for perhaps the first time, and it will feel good. "Do not move. Let the wind speak. That is paradise," wrote Ezra Pound, deftly summing up the joys of solitude.

Solitude and the slowing down that goes hand in hand, permits—no, demands—that we perceive things differently and find more beauty, more amazement and more appreciation. Go outside and really look at a dandelion, a bumblebee, a bird's nest. Rediscover the astonishing complexity of it, the *impossibility* of it existing at all. Something within you will awaken.

It is impossible not to live better, to live deeper, when one devotes time to engage with the natural world. And by engage I mean *commune with*, not conquer. We're not going to get the benefit of what I'm describing by crashing through the brush on off-road vehicles. We need to engage it slowly, with our feet connecting us to the ground, where our breath slows and we have time to see, hear, smell and feel what is present around us, and by doing that we will find what is present inside us. We will learn "To see a world in a grain of sand, and a heaven in a wild flower," as William Blake wrote. But don't expect everyone to understand. When others fear their own solitude, they won't trust you when you demand your own. Expect resistance. Mrs. Lindbergh again:

> If one sets aside time for a business appointment, a trip to the hairdresser, a social engagement or a shopping expedition, that time is accepted as inviolable. But if one says I cannot come because that is my hour to be alone, one is considered rude, egotistical, or strange. What a commentary on our civilization, when being alone is considered suspect.

But don't let others stop you. Tell them your doctor prescribed solitude because it will help cure what ails you, and I mean that literally. In her book *Healing Spaces*,[xlviii] Dr. Esther M. Sternberg discusses scientific studies that prove what we all intrinsically know: whether we are healthy or sick, slowing down and being in the natural world is good for us, even if our connection is limited to gazing upon it through a window. Her studies proved that patients healed better and faster when they had a view from their window of nature rather than an urban landscape. Dr. Sternberg writes:

> Rather than rushing through our busy days without paying much attention to the spaces around us, we need to carve out a few moments here and there to allow ourselves to be aware of our place in the world and its place inside us. We need to allow ourselves the time to see the sun glinting off the surface of the leaves, to listen to the sound of silence and of nature. We need to stop and inhale the smell of ocean salt or the fragrance of honeysuckle on a summer's night. We need to feel the gentle touch of a spring breeze . . . Perhaps it was doing all of this that allowed those patients with views of nature to heal faster than those whose views were of a brick wall.

And accumulating scientific evidence shows that being connected to the earth can have direct health benefits. The burgeoning science of "grounding" suggests, with studies to back it up, that having our bodies planted firmly on the earth provides a source of healthy electrons that shield us from detrimental environmental electric fields, helping ease arthritis, hypertension, sleep apnea and PMS, among other things.[xlix] Dr. Andrew Weil believes many of us suffer from "nature-deficit disorder," a term used to describe the damage caused to our brains and nervous systems resulting from being disconnected from the natural world. He cites the growing health problems resulting from vitamin D deficiencies caused by lack of sun exposure, vision disorders from staring at screens instead of distant vistas like the hunter-gatherers, and our failing to sleep and wake with the sun due to artificial light as examples supporting this.[l]

The Lakota tribe didn't need scientific evidence to understand the importance of being connected with Mother Earth. Here is Sioux Chief Luther Standing Bear:

> It was good for the skin to touch the earth, and the old people liked to remove their moccasins and walk with bare feet upon the sacred earth . . . The soil was soothing, strengthening, cleansing, and healing. That is why the old Indian still sits upon the earth instead of propping himself up and away from its life-giving forces. For him, to sit or lie upon the ground is to be able to think more deeply and to feel more keenly; he can see more clearly into the mysteries of life and come closer in kinship to other lives about him.

Make some time, every day if possible, and go outside, by yourself, and be still. We all need the space, the quiet, and the time alone with nature. When my mother was going through her cancer experience, she would work in her flowerbeds as long as her body would permit, and when she didn't have the strength to put her hands in the dirt, she would sit in her garden, resting, for hours. When a deacon from her former church visited her to encourage her to rejoin before it was too late, she politely told him she felt closer to God in her garden than in his church. And I do, too.

Once I was hiking in Telluride, Colorado on a solitary trip I made to re-ground myself. I take hiking trips with friends and enjoy the companionship, but that's not what I needed this time. I needed to silence the outer world to hear my inner voice. We all need this from time to time. I had found that my day-to-day living had begun to sap my creative energies, and I knew that solitude is required for creativity to have the space and time to flow from within. Driving through the mountain passes, stopping when something awed me, no one but myself to entertain me. The final two days of the trip I spent at a meditation and yoga retreat in the Rocky Mountains. I returned refreshed and inspired. I prioritize such trips, but sometimes going far away is not possible or even necessary. The writer Anne Lamott accomplishes this without leaving her home. When life becomes too frantic or stressful, she'll take what she calls a "couch cruise" where she piles up her pillows, comforter, books and magazines on her couch, nestles in, and lets everything go. It resets and heals her, she wrote. I agree. The first time I tried this, I struggled getting over the guilt that I ought to be doing something *productive*. And then I realized I was.

Quiet contemplation is needed to reconnect our hearts to our minds to our souls. Without it we are chronically preoccupied, living a surface existence. "I lived in solitude in the country and noticed how the monotony of a quiet life stimulates the creative mind," wrote Albert Einstein. Tom Hodgkinson agrees. "Long periods of languor, indolence and staring at the ceiling are needed by any creative person in order to develop ideas," he wrote. I always dread the moment I first sit down to write. I stare at the blank page and know that I don't have anything to say. But if I am patient, if I am quiet, if I am still...things begin to flow. I begin to flow. I become connected and present, and an hour goes by in what feels like minutes. This doesn't happen when I'm checking my voicemail or Facebook page.

We need to shake the idea that doing nothing is the same thing as wasting time. If you avoid work or problems by slipping into a stupor in front of a digital screen, that is wasting time. But if you are affirmatively choosing to outwardly do nothing, you are affirmatively choosing to inwardly go exploring. And big things come from that. Here is Brenda Ueland:

> So you see the imagination needs moodling,-long inefficient, happy idling, dawdling and puttering. These people who are always briskly doing something and as busy as waltzing mice, they have little, sharp, staccato ideas, such as: "I see where I can make an annual cut of $3.47 in my meat budget." But they have no slow, big ideas.[li]

Solitude is required for us to determine if what we are "busy-ing" ourselves with is how we should be spending our lives. What is the purpose in our work, our play, our relationships? These are big questions and they address the very meaning we place on our lives. It is pointless to arrive somewhere quickly if it is the wrong destination. And if you conclude you are on the right path, solitude gives you the time and space to discover if you can do what you are doing better, or can inspire a big idea or breakthrough that could change your fortune forever. Again, Lin Yutang:

> It is amazing how few people are aware of the value of solitude and contemplation. The art of lying in bed means more than physical rest for you after you have gone through a strenuous day, and complete relaxation, after all the people you have met and interviewed, all the friends who have tried to crack silly jokes, and all your brothers and sisters who have tried to rectify your behavior and sponsor you into heaven have thoroughly got on your nerves . . . If properly cultivated, it should mean a mental house-cleaning. Business men who pride themselves on rushing about in the morning and the afternoon and keeping three telephones busy all the time on their desk, never realize that they could make twice the amount of money, if they would give themselves one hour's solitude awake in bed.

And according to Michael Flocker, author of *The Hedonism Handbook*,[lii] solitude is, well, *cool*. "If you really want to indulge yourself and feel truly decadent, find a quiet spot, read a book, stare at the stars or just sit by the fire and think. Sin may be in, but silence is now in serious vogue," he wrote. I agree.

So. Solitude enlightens you, sparks your creativity, makes you healthy, wealthy, successful and cool. And yet many of us don't give ourselves this gift. But Bohemians do. And you're a Bohemian. Go find someplace quiet and think about that for a while.

You don't need to leave your room.
Remain sitting at your table and listen.
Don't even listen, simply wait.
Don't even wait.
Be quite still and solitary.
The world will freely offer itself to you.
To be unmasked, it has no choice.
It will roll in ecstasy at your feet.
Franz Kafka

Roadblocks

Every man has his own destiny: the only imperative is to follow it, to accept it, no matter where it leads him.

Henry Miller

There is a scene in the film *Vicky Cristina Barcelona* in which Vicky, the cautious, security-minded character is having dinner at a Catalonian café with her fiancé Doug and two friends from New York that they bumped into. Vicky, who had recently had a fiery one night stand with the Spanish artist and Casanova, Juan Antonio, gazes off into the distance, bored and sad, as the other three discuss home decorating and sound system installation. She sees the life ahead of her, a life of security and normality, and realizes her choice is costing her much. Her longing, her knowledge that she is *settling for*, is heartbreaking. And a warning.

Why do we make these choices? Why do we spend time half-alive, settling for nights of reality television and engagements with people whose company we don't enjoy? Why do we work unfulfilling jobs, dictated to by people we don't like or respect? Why do we continue unhappy relationships? Why do we rein ourselves in because to do what we want would break decorum, create gossip or cause embarrassment? Why do we have those random moments of clarity where we look at ourselves and say, *this can't be my life.*

We think we outgrow this. Our mothers said it didn't matter what other people thought, and we wanted to agree, but the pain and shame we felt when mocked at school for having the wrong clothes, the wrong hair or skin, the wrong *whatever* was very real. We never quite believed her. Joseph Campbell wrote that the majority of his friends were living "waste land" lives, that they had reached "the point of making the decision whether they're going to follow the way of their own zeal—the star that's dawned for them—or do what daddy and mother and friends want them to do . . . and they are just baffled."[liii] He was in his seventies when he wrote this. I doubt his friends were confused teenagers. Bonnie Ware, a hospice worker for many years, compiled a list of the top five regrets people expressed in their final weeks of life. The number one regret? "I wish I had the courage to live a life true to myself, not the life others expected of me."[15]

Often the problem is that deep down, if we admit it, we think that *they* are right, and *we* are wrong. The "they" are other people, singularly or collectively. Friends, parents, neighbors, pastors, PTA members, coworkers, bosses, celebrities, advertisers, pundits, the government.

They all tell you how you should live your life, tell you what a good life is, and tell you how you can be fulfilled. But, as much as you suppress it, a little tickle in your soul says: they are wrong. *That* is not what I want—*this* is what I want. But the consequences of listening to that voice are scary. Disapproval. Rejection. Exclusion.

But when studied closely, you realize that, 1) most feared consequences exist only in your head; and 2) the consequences that are true are insignificant when compared to what you gain in return.

A simple (although surprisingly difficult) way to start is by practicing Nancy Reagan's advice and just say no. No, I don't want to go to the family cookout. No, I don't want to stay late at the office. No, I don't need the new lawnmower just because my neighbor has one. You don't have to play golf every weekend with your buddies if you'd rather be gardening. Try it. Say "no." Everyone will survive and the world will continue to turn. Rather than your restraint feeling like deprivation, you'll be surprised at how freeing—how energizing—the little word "no" can be.

And everybody else? They'll get over it. And if they don't, their reaction says more about them than you. "When you are content to be simply yourself, and don't compare and compete, everybody will respect you," the Tao Te Ching tells us.[liv]

If others are angry, hurt or offended because you were honest with

---

15 For the full list, go to Bonnie's website at: bronnieware.com/regrets-of-the-dying/

them about who you are and what you want, you've clearly touched a nerve. After witnessing the devastation of an oil spill in the San Francisco Bay in 1973, John Francis decided to no longer ride in automobiles and walking became his sole means of transportation.[lv] When word got out and he began turning down others' offers for rides, they got angry and accused him of thinking he was better than they were. He eventually gave up speaking altogether because, among other things, he was tired of arguing with people about his choice. "It takes at least two people to argue just as it takes at least two people to communicate, and each person shares in the responsibility for both communication and argument," he said. He held firm though, and didn't step into a motorized vehicle again for seventeen years.

When others see you living out your true vision unapologetically, they are forced to examine their own lives and face the fact that they may not be living the life they want, and their anger and resentment stems from their fear of making their own changes. But you might be surprised at the responses you receive. Your friends might not enjoy the weekend golf outing that much either, and your decision may spark them to do something that they would rather do. And if not, that's okay. Maybe it's time to part ways. As novelist Haruki Murakami wrote, "If you take every single person who lacks much imagination seriously, there's no end to it."

Being in charge of our own destinies is ultimately the only responsible way to live.

Lin Yutang put it this way:

> The courage to be one's natural self is quite a rare thing . . . Few men who have liberated themselves from the fear of God and the fear of death are yet able to liberate themselves from the fear of man. Consciously or unconsciously, we are all actors in this life playing to the audience in a part and style approved by them.[lvi]

When we constantly follow others' rules, living our lives as they see fit instead of trusting our own instincts, we become a cog in a very unenlightened wheel. Be your own wheel, unapologetically. "If being an egomaniac means I believe in what I do and in my art or music, then in that respect you can call me that... I believe in what I do, and I'll say it," John

Lennon said. Many people did not like Lennon. But even more adored him. The life he lived and the art he created in his forty short years provided a fuller and deeper experience than most who have lived twice as long. He looked inward for his truth and he followed it. Society doesn't encourage this attitude, that's for sure. In *A Year of Living Consciously*, Gay Hendricks points out that the word *heretic* (not a word that carries many positive connotations) is derived from a word that means "to think for yourself."[lvii]

Carl Jung believed that a process of "individuation" is required to mature into a fully developed adult.[lviii] As children and teenagers, we spend our time learning to be part of a group, to fit into the collective. The maturation process requires that we recognize how our behaviors and choices have been shaped, albeit unconsciously at times, by our parents and early experiences. To be a free adult, we must experience a call to our own authenticity and become less identified with the group's ideas and behavior and more identified with our inner authority. "[A man] must return to the fundamental facts of his own being, irrespective of all authority and tradition, and allow himself to become conscious of his distinctiveness," Jung wrote. This ability to break away from the group is hard; the need to be part of the collective is like a magnet constantly pulling at us to join in. When people see you making choices that they wouldn't, it is natural for them to question or challenge you. And it is natural for you, even while defending yourself, to question your choice internally. Don't give in. Think it through, and then follow your own wisdom and instincts. A good friend of mine who was also a partner when I worked at the law firm tried hard to convince me I was making the wrong choice by leaving. He made good points, and I admit I wavered under his logic. But I stuck to what I knew was the right choice for me. A year later, he left, too.

A happy, confident, inspired person is a magnet for others who want to feel the same way. When I decided to take my desire to be a writer seriously, I attended a weeklong writers' workshop where I met creative people who shared the same aspirations and love of the written word that I do. They are some of my closest friends today, years later. We are mutually supportive, encouraging, and are there to remind each other we are not crazy or alone in our desire to make up stories all day.

As long as we let others make our choices for us, we are like children expecting to be rewarded and punished on our parents' whims. "We need to be responsible for ourselves; we must create our own republics," Tom Hodgkinson writes in the brilliant *How To Be Idle*.[lix] "Today we hand over our responsibility to the boss, to the company, to government, and then blame them when everything goes wrong." Others have the duty to make decisions that are best for them, but not you. It is insanity to expect someone to make your decisions for you, and if you allow it, the price you pay is steep. "Literature is strewn with the wreckage of men who have minded beyond reason the opinions of others," noted Virginia Woolf. Fail if you must, but fail on your own terms. Even if you don't reach the heights of success you desire, if you followed your own path you never really fail because you are free. True freedom is an achievement few ever gift to themselves. To do so is to be a success. You can be yourself and be part of a community. You can love and give to your family and friends without sacrificing your individuality. There is a middle road; strike the balance.

The next bully we must conquer is the popular media. The media acts much like a desperately needy person who follows us around alternately whining and screaming until we stop and give him our attention. And it works: most of us don't comprehend the level of influence the media has on what we think we want. We sneer at commercials, telling ourselves we know better than to buy in. But do we really? Marketers are clever people and they work on us in subtle ways, sometimes with devastating effects. Wilson Bryan Key, in *Subliminal Seduction*,[lx] explains how it works:

> If we assume that people are not stupid, they must react to TV commercials with a feeling of superiority that permits them to believe that they are in control. As long as this illusion persists, they would consciously have nothing to fear from commercials. People are prone to trust anything over which they believe they have control . . . An effective TV commercial is purposely designed to insult the viewer's conscious intelligence, thereby penetrating his defenses.

We think we have control, therefore we trust. Devious and brilliant.
All this spending creates debt that keeps you tied to the life you don't

want. Sure, the glossies will keep you updated on the latest and greatest, but heed the great Jack Kerouac: "Great things are not accomplished by those who yield to trends and fads and popular opinion." Let it go. The best way to fight the constant stream of consumerism and information overload is to ignore it. Turn it off and tune it out. Yes, we have a responsibility to be informed and engaged citizens. But one can ignore 90% of the media and still be both. Most of the so-called "news" is not enlightening, informing or wise, but is as damaging as advertising. Ram Dass once wrote that he went away for a few months and when he returned, he was able to catch up on all the important news in a few minutes.[lxi] The rest was trivial. Just because we have twenty-four hour news stations doesn't mean we have twenty-four hours worth of news. Most television news today is merely vinegar and sugar: it pulls you in with fear, conflict and titillation, but with no real substance underneath.

"The art of knowing is knowing what to ignore," Rumi wrote. Practice that art. And when you do check in, *read* your news. The print media, whether it is the paper, a magazine, or legitimate online source, is much more apt to stick to the facts, or, if an editorial, it can be at best thoughtful and dignified, and at worst, quiet. No so-called experts yelling at each other trying to score the best sound bite. Start a revolution by giving up your unhealthy relationship with TV. If you think you are above the influence of television and its advertisers, that you are laughing along with them, wise to their games, you're wrong.

In *Supernormal Stimuli*, Harvard evolutionary psychologist Deirdre Barrett explained that our human instincts were designed for hunting and gathering on the savannahs of Africa ten thousand years ago and our ability to evolve has not kept up with the rapid changes in our society.[lxii] Our instincts, she writes, direct us to pay attention to any sudden or novel stimulus such as a movement or sound so that we can detect and assess potential predators, prey, enemies and mates. When we encounter such a stimulus our "blood vessels to the brain dilate, those to the muscles constrict, the heart slows, and alpha waves are blocked for a few seconds," she reports. We have the same response to the television when it is on, even when we don't want to.

Truly scary, as Barrett reports, is that television draws more upon our social instincts than actual people and real events do. We'd rather watch people interact and experience life on TV than to engage in life ourselves. Barrett writes:

> *Friends* brought into our living room a group of lively roommates, whose smiles, quips, and laughter caught us up in their camaraderie without our having to exercise any social effort. *Sex and the City* gave us more vicarious romantic adventures than we'd encounter in a lifetime. In both, svelte characters noshed constantly without gaining weight; viewers joined in the eating from their own couches with quite a different outcome . . . Yet each one, after thirty to sixty minutes of the illusion of social contact, left you no richer in real friendship or family ties.

Most importantly, if you are going to be Bohemian, you *don't have the time* for much TV. You will be too busy creating, dreaming, and living. And before I'm accused of being a prohibitionist who sneaks nips from a well-hidden flask, I admit I watch TV. But like alcohol, TV is a pleasure that can become addictive and must be consumed in small doses. I watch my soccer games and check in with a few shows from time to time, and that's it. Be discerning. Yes, there are many worthwhile and enriching shows on television, but are watching them more important than painting your masterpiece or playing in the snow with your kids? Making a commitment to limit your television time is difficult, but essential. Many of the Bohemians I interviewed do not have cable television or even televisions at all. The writer Jonathan Franzen kept his clunky, old television in his closet, where he could only get a good picture by sitting cross-legged in front of it while holding the antenna. "It's hard to make TV viewing more unpleasant than I did," he wrote.[lxiii] But that wasn't enough. He ended up giving his TV away because with it around, he, a National Book Award winner and Pulitzer Prize nominee, wasn't reading books. Such is the power of television.

If you decide that what you gain from TV is too valuable to give up, try going on a media fast for a week. This hiatus will free your eyes from strain, your mind from distraction and your heart from unnecessary anxiety. View it as a soul detox that will allow you to maintain balance and control when you turn the television back on. You might find you didn't miss TV as much as you thought you would.

So much of our time is squandered consuming trivia and television is the supplier. The deeper, more poignant and more fulfilling things in life tend to be silent, waiting for you to come to them. "It is difficult to get the news from poems, yet men die miserably everyday for lack of what is found there," William Carlos Williams said. And he's right. Take his advice: the next time you are drawn to pick up a glossy magazine or turn on a reality show, pick up a book of poetry instead. Open it up on your lap and be still with it. See what the words have to tell you, and see if you regret your choice. You'll be one step closer to avoiding the miserable death Williams has rightly warned us of.

Once we've relieved ourselves of the very convincing, albeit fictitious, obligations and wants that others and the media push upon us, there's one bully left to confront: ourselves. Never underestimate a human's ability for self-inflicted suffering. We all are neurotic enough to take pleasure in our suffering from time to time, and for some of us this neurosis is a way of life. Eckhart Tolle writes that many of us are afraid to let go of our unhappiness because it makes up so much of our personality that without it we wouldn't know who we are.[lxiv]

It's time to give up the martyrdom and accept responsibility for creating our own happiness. Steve Jobs once said that every morning he looked in the mirror and asked himself, "If today were the last day of my life, would I want to do what I am about to do today? And whenever the answer has been 'No' for too many days in a row, I know I need to change something." He refused to live uninspired and so should you. Practice the skill of creative exploration and you will find it possible to rid yourself of the disease of boredom and ennui. Start with the little things. When stuck in traffic, waiting on a delayed flight in an airport or standing in line, think of stories to write or new businesses to create. Meditate. Pull a book or a journal from your pocket. Or just watch.

I know, easier said than done. But practice. If we are aware and take time to look around, inspiration lies everywhere. "If your daily life seems poor, do not blame it, blame yourself, tell yourself you are not poet enough to call forth its riches," Rainier Maria Rilke wrote. You are poet enough. Give yourself over to it. No one is too busy to stop and reflect and gather in the day's beauty, most of which is free for the taking. Believing we have too much to do is grandiose thinking and a misunderstanding of our own importance. Believing we are too poor to enjoy the day's beauty is self-inflicted blindness.

The demands of daily life can make it difficult to find the rapture of being alive, as Joseph Campbell put it, but no one is so overwhelmed that we can't exercise our sense of wonder some part of the day, every day. Thoreau wrote, "Most men live lives of quiet desperation and go to the grave with their song still in them." If you risk being one of these people, only you can change that. It's your responsibility and now is the time.

Part III

Art

If you feel like singing a song
And you want other people to sing along
Just sing what you feel
Don't let anyone say it's wrong

And if you're trying to paint a picture
But you're not sure which colors belong
Just paint what you see
Don't let anyone say it's wrong

Jeff Tweedy

It's Not Too Late

Ever since the age of six I have had a mania for drawing the forms of objects. Towards the age of fifty I published a very large number of my drawings, but I am dissatisfied with everything which I produced before the age of seventy. It was at the age of seventy-three I nearly mastered the real nature and form of birds, fish, plants, et cetera.
Consequently, at the age of eighty, I shall have got the bottom of things; at one hundred, I shall have attained a decidedly higher level which I cannot define, and at the age of one hundred and ten every dot and every line from my brush will be alive. I call on those who may live as long as I to see if I keep my word.

Signed, formerly Hokusai, Now the Painting Crazy Man[ilxv]

Prior to the start of my first grade school year, my teacher, Bobbie Starns, a Harvard graduate with unconventional attitudes about teaching, inspired the class's parents to build a clubhouse on stilts in the center of the classroom, which she filled with comic books, crayons, paint and construction paper. My father reminded me that we didn't call it a "clubhouse," it was the *Superheroes' Secret Headquarters*. When students finished assignments or had earned some special recognition, they were permitted to play in the Secret Headquarters. It was Eden to us, and we didn't require much encouragement to be diligent in our studies. Little did we care that we were teaching ourselves to read by poring over the comics and expanding our creativity and learning ability with the drawing, painting, and story writing that went on in that magical space. I wrote my first book in the Secret Headquarters, a book that Ms. Starns diligently laminated for me so that I would have a "hard back" edition. At that time, I was a writer, an illustrator, a painter, and many other things.

My family moved and I attended a different school the following year. When it came to art, group projects were important to my new teacher, and we were often given preprinted designs to mimic or to cut and paste together. Bats for Halloween. Reindeer for Christmas. Having a high value on creative independence instilled in me by my parents and Ms. Starnes, I always asked for permission to make my own bats and reindeer. For a while she allowed me, but one day her patience ran out and she scolded me, saying, "Can't you ever do what everyone else is doing?" I was shocked and crushed. I didn't ask again. I cut and pasted the preprinted designs from then on.

And so it begins.

Little by little our individuality and our creative expression is attacked, belittled, and dismissed. Pretty soon we learn that we are not talented after all, and it wouldn't matter if we were because such things aren't important in the real world. We may be pacified, even encouraged when young, but eventually we are told that the time has come to put away childish things and to grow up.

Robert Fulghum wrote of the difference in attitude that he saw in kindergartners and college students regarding what they were capable of doing. When he asked kindergartners whether they could sing, dance, draw, act, almost every child raised his hand to each thing. Of course they can draw. Of course they can sing. When he asked a roomful of college students the same question, one or two students tentatively raised a hand indicating, possibly, maybe, that they might be slightly gifted at a particular talent, but only as an amateur, of course. At six years old, they can do everything. At twenty, they can't do anything. Twenty years old, and already they ruled out so many possibilities. I'm not saying that if at age thirty you run to your mother with your drawing of a stick figure you should expect the same praise that she gave you when you were four. Expectations and standards rise, of course, as we mature. To achieve competency, much less expertise, requires much time and effort, and most of us find that we are better suited at certain creative pursuits more than others. But why do we give up so many things so early? Educator Ken Robinson believes the reason is that children are not afraid to be wrong, but by the time they reach adulthood, they lose this capacity.[lxvi] Our education system values left-brained activities more than creative pursuits, and tells us very early there is a right way and a wrong way to do things. Two plus two always equals four. To create something original, Robinson argues, we must be comfortable with being wrong often, and that comfort is not encouraged in society, or often tolerated.

Psychologist Howard Gardner's study, *The Arts and Human Development*,[lxvii] found that in painting, literature and music a normal child of seven or eight is already able to appreciate artistically as well as most adults, but imaginativeness and sensitivity in the aesthetic realm starts to wane around the age of ten and continues to decrease through adolescence. "Many children come to the threshold of artistic flowering and then fall away. Around puberty there is a 'universal change' from natural participation in artistic behavior to inhibition, abstract thought, and a failure of creative enjoyment," writes John Carey, citing the study.[lxviii] Picasso didn't need a study to know this. "All children are artists," he said. "The problem is how to remain an artist once he grows up."

Another question might be: why is it a problem at all? The answer to this question is depressing in its underlying causes. We fail to remain artists because someone convinced us art is frivolous, childish and a waste of time. Others convinced us that they knew better than us what we should value and pursue, and that they knew the extent of our talent before it unfolded. And we believed them. And this mistaken belief runs very deep within us. We think we came to this conclusion ourselves. Go look at that group of kindergartners raising their hands knowing they can do anything, and think again.

The good news is that you can change the way you think about this. You can reevaluate your opinion of your talents, their value, and your need to nurture them. It's not too late. Even if you weren't good at something when you were younger doesn't mean you can't be now. Recent brain plasticity studies have shown that our ability to learn new things does not diminish with age and that creativity can be learned. The idea that "you can't teach an old dog new tricks" has been disproved.[lxix]

Even if we never lost touch with what we love doing, we often set it aside in our mad rush for material success. We comfort ourselves with the illusion that we will make our money first, and when we are secure, we will make time for the things that fulfill us. The sad reality is that this rarely happens. Security, as we've covered, is an illusion never quite reached. And if we do reach a place of "security," often our creative expression has been dormant for so long that we've forgotten how much we loved it, how much joy it brought to our lives. If this applies to you, it's time to rediscover this love.

As George Eliot said, it's never too late to be who you might have been. If you are twenty, start now. If you are seventy, start now. Don't prejudge your talents or your capacity for success; redefine what talent and success mean. "No matter what our age or your life path, whether making art is your career or your hobby or your dream, it is not too late or too egotistical or too selfish or too silly to work on your creativity," writes Julia Cameron. "'I'm too old' is something we tell ourselves to save ourselves from the emotional costs of the ego deflation involved in being a beginner."

In our youth-obsessed culture, the media loves to indulge in stories of young "prodigies" and the next wave of "new young talent." They seldom report on the grandmother's cutting edge art. Somebody actually went to the trouble of studying the statistics to show that a new writer is more likely to be struck by lightning than to publish a novel after the age of seventy. This gives us the impression that after a certain age, we have no chance of success, and that is a false belief. When Julia Cameron was asked by a student in her creativity classes if she, "Know[s] how old I will be by the time I learn to play the piano/act/paint/write/a decent play?" she responds, "Yes...the same age you will be if you don't." She's right. Get going. At the risk of overindulgence, below is a list of a few of the *many* who have achieved success well after their "youth" had slipped into the past:

Anna Mary Robertson, aka "Grandma" Moses, was in her seventies when she began painting scenes of her rural life in upstate New York. This self-taught artist, mother and widow became one of the most famous American folk artists of the 20th century and continued painting into her nineties.

Billy Collin's first book, The Apple that Astonished Paris, wasn't published until he was in his forties. His subsequently published book, Sailing Alone Around the Room, sold almost

Joseph Downing

200,000 copies, more than any other book of poetry so far this century.lxx

Louise Nevelson was in her fifties when she sold her work to three New York City museums and now her art can be seen internationally in over eighty public collections. Shortly before her sixtieth birthday, she became President of the Artist's Equity New York chapter which was the first of many art leadership positions she attained.

When she was just shy of her fiftieth birthday, Julia Child collaborated on her first book, Mastering the Art of French Cooking. Soon after, she promoted her book on television and became a sensation in the culinary world.

Charles Darwin was fifty when he published his complete theory of evolution in On the Origin of Species, which sold out the first day it was released and subsequently had six editions.

Hungarian André Kertész spent years in France photographing artists before he immigrated to the U.S. He didn't receive recognition until the age of seventy when he had a solo show at the Museum of Modern Art. He subsequently was exhibited in galleries all over the world.

Poet Sharon Olds had been writing poetry for ten years when at age thirty she realized she was unhappy with her poems because her style mimicked other poets and did not reflect her own voice. She visited the library at Columbia University, her alma mater, and "made a deal with the devil": she would give up all she had learned there if she could write her own poems, whether they were good or not. Seven years later and a few days short of her fortieth birthday, she published her first collection, Satan Says. She said, "I was a later bloomer, but anyone who blooms at all, ever, is very lucky." She has published eight collections since.lxxi

Marilyn French was almost fifty when she published her first novel, The Women's Room. It sold more than twenty million copies and was translated into twenty languages, and was considered one of the most influential novels of the second-wave feminist movement.lxxii

Rodney Dangerfield achieved no success in show business until age forty-two. Prior to that he struggled as a writer and a comedian and supported himself by selling aluminum siding.

Jazz singer Al Jarreau's first album wasn't released until he was thirty-eight.

Poet Charles Bukowski's first book wasn't published until he was forty-nine.

Laura Ingalls Wilder's first book, Little House in the Big Woods wasn't published until she was sixty-five. She went on to write seven (yes, seven! All after the age of sixty-five!) more volumes of her Little House series.

Comic book legend Stan Lee was in his early forties when he created Spider-Man and most of his other legendary superheroes. His partner, artist Jack Kirby, started drawing The Fantastic Four when he was forty-four.

Raymond Chandler didn't publish his first short story until he was forty-five and his first novel, The Big Sleep, came out when he was fifty-one.

Sixty-five-year-old Blues guitarist Daddy Mack Orr worked as an auto mechanic until age forty-five when he decided he wanted to learn to play the guitar. Within three years he was playing gigs in Memphis and has since recorded four records, traveled across America and Europe, and jammed with Keith Richards and Ron Wood.

Joseph Conrad didn't begin seriously writing until he was thirty-six and did not become successful with a wider audience until his novel Chance came out when he was fifty-six. By then two of his best books – Lord Jim and Nostromo – had also been published.

James Michener didn't write his first novel until age forty-two and then produced a gazillion bestsellers before he died at age ninety.

What are the lessons of these later-in-life successes? One is that to develop your talent requires *a long time and a lot of work*, what writer John Gardner calls "The value of painstaking—almost ridiculously painstaking—work." According to the research of Malcolm Gladwell, we are all late-bloomers; there is no such thing as a "prodigy." In *Outliers*,[lxxiii] his work on why some people succeed more than others, he discovered what he described as the "10,000-hour rule." He found that to be really good at something, to be an expert or to rise to the top in areas with extreme competition such as the arts, sports, and industry, it takes 10,000 hours (the equivalent of three hours a day for ten years) of practice and training to get there. If you have a minimum amount of ability, the rest just requires time, perseverance and effort. Citing a study done by psychologist K. Anders Ericsson on classical music students at Berlin's Academy of Music, Gladwell writes:

The striking thing about Ericsson's study is that he and his colleagues couldn't find any "naturals," musicians who floated effortlessly to the top while practicing a fraction of the time their peers did. Nor could they find any "grinds," people who worked harder than everyone else, yet just didn't have what it takes to break the top ranks. Their research suggests once a musician has enough ability to get into a top music school, the thing that distinguishes one performer from another is how hard he or she works. That's it. And what's more, the people at the very top don't work just harder or even much harder than everyone else. They work much, *much* harder.

More interesting is Gladwell's conclusion that the so-called prodigies aren't necessarily born with exceptional talents, but worked equally hard starting at an earlier than average age. He uses the example of Mozart, who is widely known to have started writing music at age six. But none of Mozart's works produced prior to age twenty-one are considered remarkable. Only after practicing for ten years did he produce his first masterwork, Concerto No. 9, K. 271. When I interviewed novelist Katrina Kittle, I noted that it took her ten years as a professional writer before she could fully support herself from her writing alone.

Nobel Prize winning author Gabriel Garcia Marquez has acknowledged this as well. "In my case, being a writer is an exceptional achievement because I am very bad at writing. I have to subject myself to an atrocious discipline in order to finish half a page after eight hours of work," he has said.

The stories we read about "overnight success" make for good copy, but are seldom true. Writing in *The New Yorker*, Gladwell provides the example of Ben Fountain.[lxxiv] Fountain had been an associate in a law firm for several years when he decided he wanted to write fiction. At first he tried to write after he got home from work, but found that he was too tired to do so. He eventually quit his job, set up a rigorous schedule and wrote every day, writing short stories and a novel that he decided wasn't good enough and put in a drawer. He then wrote a story that was published in *Harper's* and that got the attention of an agent, who got him a book deal for a collection of short stories entitled *Brief Encounters with Che Guevara*. The collection won the Hemingway Foundation/PEN award, was named a No. 1 Book Sense Pick, was named one of the best books of the year by the *San Francisco Chronicle*, the *Chicago Tribune*, and *Kirkus Reviews*. An overnight success story? Not quite. Here is Gladwell:

> Ben Fountain's rise sounds like a familiar story: the young man from the provinces sudden-
> ly takes the literary world by storm. But Ben Fountain's success was far from sudden. He quit his
> job at Akin, Gump in 1988. For every story he published in those early years, he had at least thirty
> rejections. The novel that he put away in a drawer took him four years. The dark period lasted for
> the entire second half of the nineteen-nineties. His breakthrough with "Brief Encounters" came in
> 2006, eighteen years after he first sat down to write at his kitchen table. The "young" writer from
> the provinces took the literary world by storm at the age of forty-eight.

As a child, Anne Packard showed talent as a painter but in spite of this, her parents would not permit her to attend art school and instead forced her into the more "realistic" choice of secretarial school. Only after a marriage, five children and a divorce did she pursue her artistic career. She began selling her work in order to support her family and did so by attending every church show and art fair she could find, selling her paintings for five dollars each. On one such occasion, the renowned abstract-expressionist Robert Motherwell bought some of her paintings and helped launch her career. She believes artistic talent "Is really only five percent ability. I was a lousy painter thirty to forty years ago, but I loved reaching for something. Now, after forty years, many things just develop out of me." Time, patience, hard work, and the 10,000-hour rule. And maybe a little bit of luck thrown in, but we can always make our own luck.

Another powerful example of later-in-life success that followed great struggle is that of the painter Matisse. In *The New Criterion*, Kenneth Wayne described Matisse's journey:

> Matisse's involvement with the world of art did not come easily. . . Matisse was still tak-
> ing art classes at age thirty, at the Académie Julian where he was heckled by the younger students
> as an out-of-place old timer. Indeed, it appears that few people had high hopes or expectations
> for Matisse . . . People in his town thought he was an imbecile, a failure who was confirming
> everyone's worst fears. Matisse himself was plagued by self-doubts and a lack of confidence exac-
> erbated by his father's concerns about his abilities. Matisse did not have visions of grandeur, only
> hopes of eking out a living. His career as an artist was not truly launched until 1905, when he was
> thirty-five years old.[lxxv]

Think about that: he was told he was too old; he was called an imbecile and a failure; his father disapproved of him. And yet he kept at it. How many of us would do that? It is important to note that he kept at it *despite* being plagued by self-doubts and low confidence. As Rollo May wrote, "Courage doesn't mean the absence of despair; rather it meant the capacity to move ahead in spite of despair." Matisse is an excellent example of this. Are you that strong? Am I? We must ask ourselves these questions every day of our lives. It's easy to give up. Remember the brave ones that didn't and draw strength from them. And if you have given up, or maybe have just delayed starting, get going.

Australian artist Nona Burden is an inspiration to late bloomers. Burden graduated from law school in her late twenties and began working as a civil litigation lawyer. She got married in her late thirties and had a daughter at age forty-one. Then she decided to pursue her dream of going to art school, which she completed at the Adelaide Central School of Art.

Now in her fifties, she has had many solo shows and exhibited in London and other major cities. She didn't start until she was forty-one (remember, Matisse was considered too old at age thirty) and she succeeded. Here is Gladwell one more time:

> On the road to great achievement, the late bloomer will resemble a failure: while the late bloomer is revising and despairing and changing course and slashing canvases to ribbons after months or years, what he or she produces will look like the kind of thing produced by the artist who will never bloom at all . . . Whenever we find a late bloomer, we can't but wonder how many others like him or her we have thwarted because we prematurely judged their talents.

Sometimes achieving early success can be a curse rather than a blessing. James Murphy of LCD Soundsystem had a chance to be a staff writer on a TV pilot that he turned down, choosing instead to work on his true calling, music. (He eventually obtained success after years of being in the music business.) The pilot was for *Seinfeld*, the most successful television show in history. In an interview on *Sound Opinions*, he said he views his decision to turn down the opportunity as the right one, even though it resulted in delayed recognition by the broader world by years. "I think I would have been a real jerk because I was twenty-two and a narcissistic egomaniac," he said. "Failing consistently through my twenties set me up to be a much happier person later in life. I look at us now as a band and so much of what we are about is not being at a vulnerable age. It's about being forty. It's about being much older than you are supposed to be in a rock band."

Don't let anyone prejudge your talents. Only you know what is worth your efforts and what value you derive from what you create. If others enjoy it and benefit from it, all the better. But don't create for them and don't let them decide whether your creations are worthy or not. Do not give up. That's not the Bohemian way. It takes patience and it's never too late to start. But there's no time to wait, either.

There's No Time to Wait

She said life's too short to worry
Life's too long to wait
Life's too short not to love everybody
And life's too long to hate
I meet a lot of men who haggle and finagle all the time
Trying to save a nickel or make a dime
Not me, no sireee, I ain't got the time

"The Devil's Backbone Tavern" by Todd Snider

"GATHER YE ROSEBUDS WHILE YE MAY," wrote Robert Herrick, and we should do well to listen to him. One of my biggest regrets is one that most of us share: the amount of time wasted waiting around for some external event to change in my life that will allow me to do what I want and make me happy. Oh how the years slip through our fingers! Even now I worry and fret, thinking as soon as I pay off this or that debt, I will have the time to write the way I *really* want to. In college, I was so worried that I wasn't going to land a job and that I was going to be poor that I missed out on much of the freedom and joy that comes from a time in your life when you're allowed to be poor; when so much is available that doesn't require vast sums of money. This fearful reluctance is always lurking around the corner for me, like Gollum hounding Frodo through the swamps, and I must from time to time tell myself *enough* and get on with things. "Life, as it is called, is for most of us one long postponement," Henry Miller said. How sad, and yet how true. What are you postponing? Right now is the time to decide. When I think of this question, I sit down and I write, pushing all else aside, and I feel much better. Or instead of taking care of one of the endless never-ending streams of petty tasks that require completion I stop, take a moment and meditate. Determine what it is your soul requires. Once you have that knowledge, follow it. Express it every day. Your time is short, my friends.

When I fall in love with a book I can't help but push it on everyone, including friends whose annual reading is limited to the backs of their cereal boxes over breakfast. The response I inevitably receive is, "I would love to read more, but I just don't have the time." I can't help but think, how is that so? We both have twenty-four hours in a day; we both have seven days a week.

I learn later this person with no time watches twenty hours of television a week. How often have you said you would like to read more, write more, play more, but you just don't have time? It's time to bury that excuse, and if you need a reason why, look to William Carlos Williams. Williams was a doctor who practiced his profession for over forty years, delivering over two thousand babies in that time. And he still found time to write short stories, poems (over twenty volumes), plays, novels, critical essays, an autobiography, translations and correspondence, and be the mentor and inspiration to some of the most recognized Bohemians we know, including Allen Ginsberg. I don't think he watched much TV, though.

When a person says, "I don't have the time" to do something, what she means is, "I don't value that activity enough to prioritize it over other things in my life." Sometimes that's not only okay—it's the right thing to do. You probably should prioritize going to work over catching up with all the daytime soap operas. I'm not advocating selfishness or always placing your own needs over your family's, but I am challenging you to look at how you spend each hour of your day and compare it to what you truly value. How well did you line up? How much time are you giving to your life purpose and to what fulfills you deeply? If you are like most, I imagine a tremendous gap exists between your activities and your values.

I'm sure you've heard the saying that no one looks back on her life from her deathbed wishing she had worked more. But nor will she say she wished she'd spent more time watching television, playing video games, surfing the Internet, or shopping. But she will say she wished she spent more time doing what she loved.

Try this test: for one week, track every moment of each day in a journal and how you spent each minute. At the end of the week, separate the entries into sleep, work, eating, relaxing, wasting time, and time spent seeking fulfillment and your life purpose. Don't confuse escapist and mind-numbing behaviors with relaxing, and don't confuse relaxing with wasting time. You need down time, but you don't need to be anesthetized. Then, write down as specifically as possible your life purpose and what your values and priorities are in descending order. Based on time spent, categorize how you spent your time compared to your list of priorities. How well did you do? If you are like me, probably not as well as you hoped. But when I do this, I become more aware and I adjust my activities to better meet my values. And then I get lazy and I have to adjust again. This exercise isn't intended to make you feel guilty or anxious, just to help bring you back to your authentic self. Addictive behaviors, whether it is staying up late watching TV and then sleeping-in instead of engaging in your hour of writing before work, or eating a box of donuts to distract us from loneliness instead of meditating, ultimately causes us unhappiness.

"What'll we do with ourselves this afternoon? And the day after that, and the next thirty years?" F. Scott Fitzgerald once asked. Answer that question for yourself. Map out an average week based on how you would like to spend it. Tape it to the refrigerator and put it in action. After a few months, see how you are doing. Some weeks will be better than others, but overall, if you remain conscious of your values, you will see old patterns break, new patterns emerge, and one day you will wake up feeling better about everything in your life without needing to pin down exactly why. Escapist activities such as watching television or shopping are okay from time to time; we all do it and enjoy it. But these activities do not truly fulfill us yet we allocate our time as if they do. Reevaluate. Reprioritize. Turn off the television more often. You will not—I guarantee—regret on your deathbed all the shows you missed.

Insane in the Right Brain

But you'd be surprised when you're put right on the ball and you've got to do something and everybody's looking at you, going, OK, what's going to happen? You put yourself up there on the firing line—give me a blindfold and a last cigarette and let's go. And you'd be surprised how much comes out of you before you die. Especially when you're fooling the rest of the band, who think you know exactly what you're going to do, and you know you're blind as a bat and have no idea. But you're just going to trust yourself. Something's going to come.[lxxvi]

Keith Richards

Art washes away from the soul the dust of everyday life.

Pablo Picasso

The American painter and illustrator N.C. Wyeth lived his life as if he was a character in one of his many great paintings. His children remembered him being so engrossed in his art that if he were painting a knight swinging a sword, N.C.'s arm would hurt from the weight of the sword as if he were the one swinging it.[lxxvii] His love of creative expression was contagious, spreading to all his children. His home became an artistic paradise.

He and the kids wrote plays and created their own elaborate stages and costumes. He read stories of adventure to them every night. His son Nat remembered an evening N.C. took his children to see the film *Mutiny on the Bounty*. When the film ended and the patrons were leaving, N.C. pulled his kids close and said, "Turn around and look at all these people coming out of the theater. Did you ever see a duller bunch of faces? Look at those expressions. That's the trouble with movies. Your imagination goes to sleep." He didn't dislike movies, but he wanted to make sure his children understood the act of creation was more important than the observance of it. He was instilling in his kids the importance of imagination. And it worked.

Of his five children, three became accomplished painters and the most recognized, Andrew Wyeth, is regarded as one of the best America has produced. Another child became a composer and musician with the Philadelphia Orchestra, performing her compositions when she was only nineteen. The last, Nat, became an engineer and holds twenty-three patents, including the common soda pop plastic bottle. "In his household, being creative and being alive were one and the same thing," said historian David McCullough.

Okay. We've gotten past the idea of fame and fortune as being the driving force of doing what we love. But what's left? Why do it? It's very simple: the act of creation is its own reward. *Being creative and being alive are one and the same thing.* "The pursuit of reward is even more power-fully felt than the achievement of it," Dr. Esther M. Sternberg confirms in *Healing Spaces.* The process, the act, the experience is the goal, not the result. In the creative act, our senses are heightened, our focus narrows and our heart swells, even when the act is difficult.

And the gifts creative expression gives do not end when we put down our pen or brush. Engaging in creative activities boosts our success in other areas of our lives. In their recent investigation on creativity,[lxxviii] journalists Po Bronson and Ashley Merryman reported that studies were proving that creative people are more "engaged, motivated and open to the world." If you have children, setting an example is reason alone to express your creative side: Bronson and Merryman cite research done by Indiana University's Jonathan Plucker that found that childhood Creativity Quotient (CQ) was three times more important than Intelligence Quotient (IQ) in achieving measured success throughout a lifetime. American children's IQ and CQ had been steadily rising in the United States until around 1990, when, while IQ scores continued to rise, CQ scores began steadily dropping. Experts believe television and video games are significantly to blame. Bronson and Merryman write, "According to University of Texas Professor Elizabeth Vandewater, for every hour a kid watches television, his overall time in creative activities—from fantasy play to arts projects—drops as much as eleven percent. With kids spending about three hours in front of televisions each day, that could be a one-third reduction in creative time—less time to develop a sense of creative self-efficiency through play."

The act of creating is spiritually enriching. If I told you to work days, weeks, even months on your masterpiece and said when you finished you had to destroy it, would you still do it? You should. That's what Tibetan Monks do when they create their beautiful sand mandalas. The mandalas, which are elaborate sand "paintings," are created and ritualistically destroyed once completed to symbolize the Buddhist belief in the transitory nature of material life. And, sooner or later, everything you create *will* be destroyed. Don't create for posterity, fame, or money. Do it for the experience of doing it. Deepak Chopra describes this as being process-oriented instead of outcome-oriented. "The sooner you lose your rigid attachment to the outcome you find you can accomplish the goal with much less effort," he says.[lxxix] "Go to the field of silence from where all creativity comes, have the desire, let go, and watch the results."

Despite having published novels and multiple short stories, writer Ed Davis has seen his share of rejections. At sixty, publication means much less to him now. He would still write if he were to never again publish. He explains:

> Writing is a sacred thing. It puts me in touch with the sources. The spirit guides. It takes me deep into my unconscious. I totally lose myself. Writing is my life. Addiction is addiction, whether the addiction is to alcohol or publication. And at one time, I was so addicted to writing as a means to fame and fortune, where publication was god, and it was very unhealthy. So I've given that up. But that's a tough one. I can't say I don't want to be published. But I'm not depending on it; I'm not expecting it. Blaming agents, editors, or others in power is toxic. Publication is great, but not necessary.

Photographer Julie Larsen shares Davis's view. Feeling creatively stagnant, Larsen returned to college at age forty-six and received a bachelor's degree in photography four years later at age fifty. She has won grants, galleries have exhibited her work and her art has sold, but she still desires the validation that comes with ongoing recognition. But the creative act alone is enough to keep her working. Her photography has changed the way she engages the world. She no longer *looks*, she *sees*. "If I walk along a beach, I now notice the patterns in the sand, how the color on one side is different from the other, how the pattern would make a good background for a painting," she said. "I watch the tide come in and see how the lines divide the sand, how the lines curve. And I want to create something from what I see." When she is out with her camera, by herself, and she captures images that interest her, she comes home with a huge sense of accomplishment. Even if she never uses the images. Such is the power of creative expression.

Unlock yourself from the chains of expectation. As the Bhagavad-Gita says, "The wise man lets go of all results, whether good or bad, and is focused on the action alone." Judeo-Christian tradition advises the same, as evidenced from the Gnostic Gospel of Thomas: "If you bring forth what is within you, what you bring forth will save you. If you do not bring forth what is within you, what you do not bring forth will destroy you." Free your creativity and be liberated. Repress it, and die under its weight. The product of what you create has value, of course, but so often the value of the act itself on our mental and physical wellbeing is undervalued. Author Fred Arment believes that artistic expression has value beyond any fame or fortune that comes from the published work. As with Davis, his writing is a spiritual practice. "Some people pray, some meditate, I write," he said. According to Bronson and Merryman, one way to increase creativity is to pose the following challenge: "Do something only you would come up with—that none of your friends or family would think of." What can you do? What can your partner and/or children do? Ask and see what happens.

When a reporter asked Bob Dylan on his 1966 tour why he sang, his answer was, "Because I feel like singing." You could interpret that as being glib, or you can interpret it as being the truest answer anyone could or should give. I believe he shared the opinion of the Indian mystic, Osho, who said:

If you really want to be creative, then there is no question of money, success, prestige, respectability—then you enjoy your activity; then each act has an intrinsic value. You dance because you like dancing; you dance because you delight in it. If somebody appreciates it—good, you feel grateful. If nobody appreciates, it is none of your business to be worried about it. You danced, you enjoyed—you are already fulfilled.

The Abundant Bohemian

Kathleen Norris tells the story of the desert Monk Abba Paul, who, like many monks, wove baskets while he prayed.[lxxx] But because his home was seven days journey through the desert to the nearest town, he had no market to sell his baskets. She writes:

> Because Paul lived at such a remove from civilization that he could not even distract himself with the notion of selling his baskets, he was forced to admit that he was engaged, day in and day out, in useless activity. As soon as he had filled his cave with baskets, he would have only to burn them and begin again. The tale is a wry comment on the futility of all human effort, and on mortality itself. There is no denying that we, like Paul's baskets, will one day be nothing but ashes. Our work is bound to be forgotten. But monks still tell Paul's story because they take heart from his perseverance and bold humility in the face of acedia. His steadfast labor at both work and prayer reminds us that even if what we do seems worthless, it is still worth doing.

Start by developing an interest in life as you see it: people, nature, literature, music—the world is rich with inspiring treasures, beautiful places and interesting people. Forget yourself for a while and soak it in.

Despite all the benefits, it's still a struggle to begin. And then begin again. I know from experience. Whether it's writing or painting, facing that blank page or canvas is daunting. The temptation to jump away to read just one more blog entry hovers in my consciousness. Maybe I should vacuum the floor first. Maybe it would be better to go to the coffee shop and write there. So many ways to cheat myself! And so many times I have, despite *knowing* how much the creative act means to me, how much I enjoy it once in the flow, and how good I feel afterward. And even more difficult, to spend two years on a novel, have it rejected, and say: now start another.

Creativity is *hard*. Anything worthwhile is. But we must choose to engage our creativity instead of following the path of least resistance. In *The Courage to Write*,[lxxxi] Ralph Keyes correctly points out that, "Getting there [writing a novel] isn't always pleasant. Neither is running in a marathon. Or starring in a play. Or climbing a mountain. All such activities require courage. And all reward those who complete them not only with an unparalleled feeling of achievement but with a thrilling sense of adventure along the way."

We are all guilty of being lazy from time to time. But do not feel guilty; become more fulfilled. What I'm hoping to curb is narcotic behavior—our desire to avoid doing what we really want to do because something slightly easier—albeit less fulfilling—happens to be available. Figure out a way to discipline yourself. Early in The Rolling Stones' career, the band only played and recorded cover songs and their manager, Andrew Oldham, decided they needed original material. He locked Mick and Keith in a kitchen and told them he wasn't letting them out until they wrote a song. They didn't believe him at first, but he held to his word. They spent the whole night in the kitchen, but they came up with "As Tears Go By." From then on, they knew they were songwriters and the rest is history. Lock yourself in your own metaphoric kitchen and get busy.

The Validation Prison

If you look to others for fulfillment,
you will never truly be fulfilled.
If your happiness depends on money,
you will never be happy with yourself.

The Tao Te Ching

Fear of rejection and the fear of ridicule are the archenemies of creative expression. The act of creating something new exposes us and we feel vulnerable. Feeling vulnerable makes us feel weak and ripe for pain. People love to be told what they did was great, but anything short often feels like a mortal wound. And this—and this alone—is the reason so many creative people give up. That is not the Bohemian way. Sometimes others won't relate to our chosen creative expression; they just won't get it. You can make the best broccoli casserole ever made, but if someone doesn't like broccoli, she's not going to like your dish. It doesn't make you a bad chef. Many people will be too distracted, too busy, or too lazy to consider your work seriously. Others may lack the talent or vision to recognize your work for what it is. This is especially true if your work is not like anything they have seen before. And in our all-or-nothing, win-at-all-costs culture, we desperately want the stamp of validation on our work. We're not writers until a New York publishing house publishes our novel. We're not painters until we have a show at a prestigious gallery. We're not musicians without a record contract.

It's time to let all that go.

Everything we create, everything we put out to the world as a form of expression, will subject us to scrutiny. If what you put out is true and meaningful to you, criticism will hurt. And you *will* be criticized. And you will be praised. Probably for the same reasons.

It is helpful to know that even the greats were subject to ridicule by their generation's self-appointed torchbearers of artistic quality. Here is John Carey, from his book *What Good Are The Arts?*:

> Shakespeare is probably the writer that most high-art advocates would select as a universally acclaimed genius, whose reputation proves that there are indeed artistic values that surmount place and time... But even among the intelligent and educated across the centuries there has never in fact been a consensus about Shakespeare's greatness. Darwin, Voltaire and Tolstoy were all disparaging... University-educated intellectuals in Shakespeare's own day such as Thomas Nashe and Robert Greene would have found the suggestion that he [Shakespeare] was a great writer utterly ridiculous. On the contrary, they described him as an 'upstart,' a semi-educated plagiarist, on the fringe of the literary world.

Hemingway may have said that *The Adventures of Huckleberry Finn* was the true great American novel, but that's not the reception Mark Twain received when it was first published in 1885. *The Boston Evening Transcript* labeled it "The veriest of trash" and the *Boston Evening Traveler* wrote, "H.F. appears to be singularly flat, stale and unprofitable. . . the taste of this gratuitous presentation is as bad as the book itself, which is an extreme statement." Most entertainingly, The Concord, Massachusetts Public Library banned the book because it was "Trash and suitable only for the slums." What if Shakespeare and Mark Twain did what many creative people do, and took this criticism seriously and stopped making their art? To do so sounds ridiculous, and it is. But yet this is the choice many of us make. Try instead to use rejection to spur you on and to inspire you.

Editors, gallery owners, record company execs, theater directors, venture capitalists—they are all going to tell you *no* at one time or another. You can take their word for it and quit, or you can move on until you find someone who believes in your art. We want so much for these large institutions to open their doors to us that we don't see that although they are quite good at knowing what *was* popular, successful, or merit worthy, they often fail when it comes to knowing what *will* be. In 1913 the first major exhibition of abstract art, the "Armory Show," opened in New York City. On display were works by Picasso, Van Gogh, Matisse, Monet, and many others. Even though over 100,000 people went to see it, it wasn't deemed a success by many of the critics at the time. Harriet Monroe, the founder of *Poetry Magazine*, described the works of Matisse as, "The most hideous monstrosities ever perpetrated on long suffering art." Teddy Roosevelt ran through the rooms waving his arms and yelling, "That's not art!" But the art sold anyway.[lxxxii] Robert Pirsig's *Zen and the Art of Motorcycle Maintenance* was rejected by 121 publishers before being accepted. It went on to sell three million copies. Decca Records turned down The Beatles for being *unmarketable.* And this rejection and criticism is not limited to new artists trying to break through. Even established artists risk ridicule if they dare challenge the public's expectations. When Diego Rivera discovered his style, he was ridiculed by the art critics of his day, who wanted him to remain a traditionalist. "Aged connoisseurs still hold [his early work] up against the later Riveras and shake their heads over his 'uglyistic' degeneration—he was once a lad of such promise!" wrote Bertram Wolfe.

"The world of galleries, dealers and patrons came to be seen as exclusive, the preserve of money and privilege," John Carey wrote of the modern history of the arts. "Museums are just a lot of lies," Picasso said, supporting this view. Yes, there are many talented, honest and passionate agents, editors and producers who work tirelessly to find and support new artists. These people care deeply, work hard, and are inundated. It is understandable that many gems slip through their fingers. But the truth of the matter is, many of the people deciding who gets contracts or gigs or exhibitions just don't know what they're doing. Don't believe them if they say what you have created is unworthy. Let's hear what the brilliant Nick Tosches has to say about the publishing industry in his novel, *In the Hand of Dante:*

> In thirty years, I had seen the publishing racket reduced to a drab, unimaginative, and unsuccessful form of corporate salesmanship that grew every day more devastating in its mediocrity . . . Six corporate entities now controlled about seventy-five percent of the adult book market; and four of these six controlled about two thirds of the market by themselves . . . The power had shifted to the business departments, whose ineffective calculations of demographics, marketing potentiality, and projected profits decided the fate of books. Books were products, and those products that

were judged, more often wrongly than not, to represent the lowest common denominator of the taste of the populace were deemed to be of the most value . . . A love of the classics might be professed, but the truth was that no editor could or would publish these books today.[lxxxiii]

Not one to mince words, that Mr. Tosches. And Joseph Campbell shared Tosches' view. He writes:

> [The United States] is a curiously unartistic country in its common character, and yet it has produced some of the greatest artists of the century. But they are not recognized publicly; those that are recognized publicly are the razzle-dazzlers who come across in the popular media . . . I don't understand those people. The things they're interested in purveying to the public seem to be of momentary sensational interest. I'm not saying they are not worthy, but why are they all running in the same direction?

But before you conclude Tosches or Campbell are merely bitter or out of touch, let's look at the example of *The Help,* by Kathryn Stockett. Sixty literary agents rejected Stockett's novel before she found someone who saw its merit. The novel went on to sell over one million hardcover copies, was named *USA Today*'s book of the year for 2009 and was subsequently made into a successful film. Sixty agents read it and decided it wasn't even worth sending on to a publisher. How many of us would have got that sixtieth rejection letter and given up? How many of us would have made it to ten?

And another example: Lisa Genova was a thirty-eight-year-old healthcare industry consultant (with a Ph.D. in neuroscience from Harvard, mind you) who couldn't get her novel, *Still Alice*, published. She queried literary agents. She went to writers' conferences and networked. She e-mailed editors. Nothing came of these efforts, so she decided to publish the book herself. One agent who turned her down told her not to do this, that doing so would ruin her writing career before it started. She published it anyway, and took on the job of promoting it herself, selling the book from the trunk of her car to whomever would buy it. And here's the thing that all those agents and editors didn't see: people liked her book. She steadily made sales. Finally someone at Simon & Schuster got a clue and bought her novel for over half a million dollars. Target, Borders, and Barnes &

Noble all chose it for their book clubs and recommended reading lists. *Still Alice* debuted at number five on the New York Times best-seller list. So much for ruining her career.

If you believe in what you have created, take your destiny in your own hands. And technology is providing ways to achieve this that weren't possible before. In a recent *Newsweek* article about the changing nature of the publishing industry, reporter Andrea Sachs discussed how a grassroots movement is taking the stain off self-publishing by noting that writers who are passed over by traditional publishers are creating new ways to find their audience.[lxxxiv] She writes:

> In theory, publishers are gatekeepers: they filter literature so that only the best writing gets into print. But . . . there are cultural sectors that conventional publishing isn't serving. We can read in the rise of self-publishing not only a technological revolution but also a quiet cultural one—an audience rising up to claim its right to act as a tastemaker too.

And claim that right we should. After all, who really has the authority to tell you your painting, your book or your band's new album is "worthy?" If someone gets something from it, it's worthy. Again, the highly respected art critic John Carey:

> When champions of high art dismiss or devalue the pleasures people get from so-called low art . . . the argument of the high-art champions will be reducible to something like this: 'the experience I get when I look at a Rembrandt or listen to Mozart is more valuable than the experience you get when you look at or listen to whatever kitsch or sentimental outpourings you get pleasure from.' The logical objection to this argument is that we have no means of knowing the inner experience of other people, and therefore no means of judging the kind of pleasure they get from whatever happens to give them pleasure. Taste is so bound up with self-esteem, particularly among devotees of high art, that a sense of superiority to those with 'lower' tastes is almost impossible to relinquish without risk of identity crisis.

High art devotees' identity crises are not your problem. If they don't like what you create, they can ignore it. And you can do the same to them if you don't like what they have to offer. Jungian psychologist and author James Hillman backs Carey up. "The literature of Western civilization since the eighteenth century mainly turns on snobbish appraisals of mediocrity, and this tradition can catch up anyone attempting to deal with the theme. No soul is mediocre . . . whatever your personal record of middling achievements," he wrote.[lxxxv]

Go ask a child if a song/painting/story has "merit" or is in "good taste." She will look at you like you are crazy. A child either likes something or doesn't. Create, find your audience however large or small, and don't worry about the rest. That's the New World Order. And if you do create something in bad taste, have fun with it. "A little bad taste is like a nice dash of paprika," Dorothy Parker said.

Despite previously achieving relative success with her band, The Runaways, Joan Jett's first solo album was rejected by twenty-three different record companies. She decided to release it on her own and her single, "I Love Rock and Roll," became a number one hit and sold over ten million copies. And we have tools today that she didn't have. Musicians are publishing their videos on YouTube, burning their own CDs, and streaming their music online. Artists are marketing their paintings through self-created websites. Writers are self-publishing their books and marketing them through blogs, podcasts, and other new ways. In *Weird Like Us*, Ann Powers argues that musicians came of age in the indie scene of the 1980s and 1990s and developed an independence from the powers-that-be that didn't exist before. "Perfecting the do-it-yourself ethic punk had introduced, indie rockers make their own records, book their own clubs, publish their own fanzines, and tour in their own vans," she wrote.

In August 2010, *Newsweek* noted the changing field of nontraditional books in its article, "Who Needs a Publisher?" Journalist Isia Jasiewicz writes, "In the DIY era, putting out your own book is no longer an act of vanity."[lxxxvi] She noted that five of the top 100 bestsellers in the Kindle offerings were self-published, and Kindle has more sales of e-books than Amazon's hardcover sales. The article highlights author J. A. Konrath who made a profit in the six figures that year publishing his thrillers as e-books, where he keeps 70% to 80% of the profits, as opposed to the traditional 8% to 9% of royalties paid in traditional publishing. Technology is providing artists new ways to get noticed, and it is working. After horror/thriller novelist Scott Sigler's novels were rejected over a hundred times, he invested $500 in recording equipment and recorded his first novel and released it, a chapter a month, for free as a podcast. By the end of the first book, 10,000 people were listening and that was enough to snare a contract with a small publisher. He did the same for his second novel, and the audience increased to 30,000. This led to a bidding war for his third novel, and he was rewarded with a three-book hardcover contract with Crown Publishing.

And we are not only talking about techy twenty-somethings. Author Barbara Bisco knew the statistics about being published after the age of seventy, but that didn't stop her. After being universally rejected by the publishing industry, she, her husband and daughter set up their own publishing company and published Bisco's novel, *A Taste for Green Tangerines*. "The more people told us that there were rules to publishing, the more we set out to break those rules . . . after a while we just started to break the rules intentionally," her daughter said. Well done.

Artist Shon Walters said he learned that being an artist pure of heart does not mean the business side will take care of itself. "I used to think as long as you made the art and you knew it was good, everything would be okay, and when in doubt just keep making the work," he told me. "But I learned how much networking and promoting your work matters." He started exhibiting outside of his home state of Ohio and organizing shows himself rather than concentrating on established galleries. He and fellow artist Eric Wright now create art exhibitions and multimedia events that initially drew around two hundred people. Each show grew exponentially, with the most recent drawing more than two thousand. These events provide an opportunity to expose his (and others') work to new patrons and to make contacts with other artists. "You can do good work, but if you stand in the corner and don't talk to anyone, you're going to miss opportunities," he said. "My sales increased dramatically once I made the leap from 'I'm going to make that work as good as I can and I don't need to talk about it' to sharing the stories of the work with people." He writes narratives describing the life of his sculptures and the work that went into creating it. "These stories get into people's heads and hearts and they have a better appreciation for the work."

Katrina Kittle agrees. Even though she has a publishing contract with a major New York house, much of the responsibility of promoting and selling her work falls on her shoulders. "People underestimate how much promotional work is required," she said. "I need to write guest blogs. I need to respond to readers. I need to constantly work at trying to get people to know who I am and about my book." DIY, folks. Don't create your art and sit back, like a child, and expect the world to embrace you. Go and embrace it.

It is also important that you don't make the mistake of believing the amount of money your art makes dispels or validates its worth. There are people creating awful stuff and making lots of money from it. And then there is Vincent Van Gogh, who made only $109 on all his paintings during his lifetime. I have heard many new writers say, "I can't wait to publish my book so that I can quit my job." I can appreciate wanting to spend all your time doing what you love, but such an expectation will lead to disappointment. Acknowledging this is not pessimistic or even pragmatic; it's choosing to focus on the love of the process and detaching ourselves from the result. It is dangerous to judge your worth by the opinion of others, whether that be publisher, studio, publicist, or purchasing audience. We can never control what happens outside of us. We can control the joy and growth we receive from our self-expression. Grab the reins and run.

But it's a mistake to think that going outside the mainstream is simple. "If you think that self-publishing your book is easy, you're not doing it right," successful author M. J. Rose has said in an interview with NPR. All the promotion and hard work needed to convince consumers to buy your product falls in your lap and your lap alone. A big reason successful self-published authors eventually sign with a major publishing house is so the publisher can take over many of these duties (but many duties remain with the author). And just because you *can* self-publish your art doesn't mean you necessarily *should*. You must be disciplined and critical enough to know that you have produced your best work and that it is ready for the marketplace. Many mistakenly release their art prematurely and are disenchanted when the world doesn't embrace it. Remember the 10,000-hour rule.

Hemingway provides a good example of this. Early in his career he and his wife, Hadley, were traveling through Europe when Hadley accidentally left on the train a trunk full of Hemingway's manuscripts. At first he was furious, but later realized it was the best thing that could have happened: his writing was not that good yet and losing the early drafts forced him to start over, rewrite, and vastly improve his stories.

The list of people going on to achieve critical and commercial success despite being rejected and ridiculed is endless. But, sadly, "others" rarely are the real obstacle. We more often sabotage and defeat ourselves before anyone else has a chance to do so.

Society teaches us early on that if we can't be the best, we shouldn't do it at all. Silver medals are for losers. Somewhere along the line while learning the adult skill of comparing and competing, we lose the ability to express pure joy through the act of doing, through the act of expressing. "One of the very worst, self-murdering lies that people tell themselves is that they are no good, have no gift and nothing important to say," writes Brenda Ueland.

The emphasis should be on the creating, not the creation. It is the act, the moment, the beingness of it that is important, and this applies to both the creator and the appreciator. Maybe the singer-songwriter in your local bar won't be the next Dylan, but he's there, in front of you, connecting with you, and that is worthy of respect regardless of whichever side of the microphone you stand. You are alive and active—not passive—and you are deciding what deserves your attention, not the marketing executives at Big Records, Inc.

And when you compare yourself to those that you admire and you come up short—and you will come up short—know that is part of the creative process, too. All artists feel this way. "The awful thing about the first sentence of any book is that as soon as you've written it you realize this piece of work is not going to be the great thing that you envision it can be," novelist Tom Wolfe wrote. Even those deemed to have achieved notable success acknowledge the reward/recognition dynamic is not black and white, but rather bittersweet and nuanced. Here is John Updike:

> There is more than one measurement of success. A slender poetry volume selling less than a thousand copies and receiving a handful of admiring reviews can give its author a pride and sense of achievement denied more mercenary producers of the written word. As for bad reviews and poor sales, they can be dismissed on the irrefutable hypothesis that reviewers and book buyers are too obtuse to appreciate true excellence. Over time, many books quickly bloom and then vanish; a precious few unfold, petal by petal, and become classics.[lxxxvii]

And what if you never break through with the mainstream? Are you a failure? Of course not. But our culture's perpetuation of what it means to be successful makes you feel like one. If you are able to do what you love you *have* succeeded, even if you have an audience of one. "A person is a success if he gets up in the morning and gets to bed at night and in between does what he wants to do," Bob Dylan said. This is still true if part of your day is spent doing other work. The key is finding time for your passion and not letting yourself or anyone else get in your way.

Redefine success. It's time to let go of the need for validation and redefine what being successful means. Brenda Ueland says this about the joy of writing, although you can substitute any act of creative passion:

> I want to assure you with all earnestness, that *no* writing is a waste of time,-no creative work where the feelings, the imagination, the intelligence must work. With every sentence you write, you have learned something. It has done you good. It has stretched your understanding. Even if I knew for certain that I would never have anything published again, and would never make another cent from it, I would still keep on writing.

Instead of waiting for approval from the music industry, at the age of nineteen, singer-songwriter Ani DiFranco started her own record label, "Righteous Babe Records," to publish her music. She owns her master tapes, and no record execs tell her what to do or how to do it. The only person to tell her "no" was herself. She did this in Buffalo, NY, not necessarily a so-called "center of culture." She was patient, happy to play in a bar for five people. She wasn't holding out for rock star status or for happiness to come in some far off date in the future.

"People have this pie in the sky definition of success," she said in an interview with *Sound Opinions* in 2009. "For me, 'successful' means I play music, I feed myself, I pay my rent. I was successful when I was 18. When young people ask me how do I get the tour bus with the curtains and the TV, I say worry about getting the next gig and the next and the next." She is now married and a mom, but still tours regularly. "Become yourself, trust yourself, love yourself, respect yourself. Not only come up with your own answers, but come up with your own questions. Don't think as others think—think as you think."

Well said, Ani.

Rediscover what you loved to do as a child, regardless of your internal critic's view of your talent. Enjoy the act, not the product. Share it or don't. Just *do*. Decide to dance, sing, write, paint, draw, sculpt, strum, build, plant, act, carve, chisel, grow, cook, brew, eat, drink, knit, skip, or _____ (fill in the blank). Pick one of the above and immerse yourself in the activity at least twice a month for an hour. It's not asking that much, nor is it selfish. You only have to pick one, and you have the option to write one in yourself. After you've been engaged with your chosen creative outlet for a month, increase it to three times a month. If you find this difficult to do, ask yourself: what am I doing with my time? What is it that keeps me so busy I don't have an hour every two weeks to write my poetry? Is what I'm otherwise doing more important? You need that time and you deserve that time. You have that time. Get to it.

Part IV

Pleasure

People of course continue to seek pleasure through shopping, drinking, and forms of prepackaged entertainment that are mildly engaging at best. But the news is out, and has been at least since the 1960s: We are capable of so much more.

Barbara Ehrenreich, *Dancing in the Streets*

Make Merry

The mystery of the means by which these light-hearted Bohemians sustained their precarious existence was not revealed to me; yet here they sat, and laughed, and talked, and recited the poetry of their own manufacture, and sang their songs, and drank, and smoked their big pipes, and rolled cigarettes incessantly, happy enough in the hour of their lives, bringing hither none of the pains and pangs and numbing evidences of their struggles.

From *Bohemian Paris of Today*,
written by W.C. Morrow & Édouard Cucuel, published 1899.

The Bohemians Morrow and Cucuel describe may have had struggles, but despite their "pains" and "pangs" one thing stands out: they seemed to really know how to have a *good time*.

More than a century later, how do we compare?

As we already know, Americans spend more time watching TV, listening to the radio, surfing the Internet and reading newspapers than anything else except breathing.[lxxxviii] "Americans have an inability to relax into sheer pleasure," writes Elizabeth Gilbert in *Eat, Pray, Love*.[lxxxix] "Ours is an entertainment seeking nation, but not necessarily a pleasure-seeking one. Americans spend billions keeping themselves amused with everything from porn to theme parks to wars, but that's not exactly the same as quiet enjoyment." The massive success of her book is evidence that many dissatisfied souls are looking for something different.

I have faith in you, good reader, that you are not one of the many people who prefer the distractions of television or video games to the living, breathing, tasty world with all its delights. "All human happiness is sensuous happiness," says our guru Lin Yutang. It's time to spread the Bohemian word, brothers and sisters, and drag people out of the cave where they're watching the shadows on the wall. It's time to become evangelically unconventional. Here is Yutang describing sensuous happiness:

The Abundant Bohemian

To me, for instance, the truly happy moments are: when I get up in the morning after a night of perfect sleep and sniff the morning air and there is an expansiveness in the lungs, when I feel inclined to inhale deeply and there is a fine sensation of movement around the skin and muscles of the chest, and when therefore, I am fit for work; or when I hold a pipe in my hand and rest my legs on a chair, and the tobacco burns slowly and evenly; or when I am traveling on a summer day, my throat parched with thirst, and I see a beautiful clear spring, whose very sound makes me happy, and I take off my socks and dip my feet in the delightful, cool water; or when after a perfect dinner I lounge in an armchair, when there is no one I hate to look at in the company and conversation rambles off at a light pace to an unknown destination, and I am spiritually and physically at peace with the world.

Compare that to an hour spent in front of the television. I believe we all in our secret hearts want to shake the shackles off our soul, throw the remote control at the Xbox and run outside and spin in circles until we fall down. But alas, we become that serious thing known as an ADULT and tell ourselves we must let go of childish things, when really we're so neurotic and status-protective that we're too scared to do anything but numb ourselves with vodka while watching *Survivor*. Even Homer Simpson can't let himself go, as he explains to Bart the realities of adulthood:

"Son, we all have to do things we don't want to. Like have jobs and families and responsibilities . . . You think I wouldn't rather be living nude in the forest like some ancient pagan dancing around playing the pan flute?"

How much happier we would all be if we could just let go and allow ourselves the freedom to experience and enjoy, even if we risk looking ridiculous. Homer would do well to follow the advice of David Deida:

How would our lives be different if we fully trusted and acted upon our intuitions and feelings? How much happier would we be if we spent more time moving with the force of life, dancing, singing, making love and walking in the woods or the garden—rather than always pushing ourselves along a path that we think is leading to where we want to go?

I have had my share of moments when I have failed to act because I was afraid of what I would look like, or when I decided, unconsciously, that it was easier to do nothing than to be rejected and fail. Fortunately,

155

I have pushed past my fear enough times, at crucial times, to know the joy that comes with following your instincts and going for it. In my early twenties I played for a soccer team sponsored by a local German social club, and in exchange we served beer and food at their annual Oktoberfest. One Oktoberfest I saw this beautiful girl sitting at a table and I couldn't take my eyes off her. Dark hair, dark eyes, olive skin, stunning smile. She caught me staring and smiled back. I froze in embarrassment. I busied myself serving brats and occasionally glanced her way. Each time she looked back with a smile, and yet I couldn't bring myself to speak to her. But as Keith Richards says, "If you don't make bold moves, you don't get fucking anywhere." In a fit of bravery, I ran over and tapped her on the shoulder, introduced myself, and asked her out. She said yes.

Angelika was an Austrian exchange student, and we spent the rest of the glorious summer together. We wrote a steady stream of letters (yes, real letters, and hers always arrived in those exotic blue international envelopes) throughout the winter, and the next summer I traveled to Austria for a study abroad program that I had chosen solely for its locale. We had another beautiful summer together—one of the best of my life—and two other students I met in the program are still my good friends today (I'm the godfather of one's child). Angelika is married with two kids in Vienna now, and we still keep in touch.

And yet, it almost didn't happen. I very easily could have said "screw it," let her walk to the car, get in and drive away, never to see her again, because I knew I might get rejected or embarrass myself. How many opportunities like this have I missed? How many have you? "We've all heard that the unexamined life is not worth living, but consider too that the unlived life is not worth examining," wrote Julia Cameron.

We work so hard to maintain respectability. To protect decorum and avoid embarrassment. To behave modestly and *moderately.* "Why then," as the Greek philosopher Epictetus wrote two thousand years ago, "do you walk as though you had swallowed a ramrod?" Because even moderation should be done in moderation. The true Bohemian must step out of his skin and his comfort zone every once in a while, if only to remind himself where his comfort zone ends. As Robert McIver says, "The healthy being craves an occasional wildness, a jolt from normality, a sharpening of the edge of appetite, his own little festival of Saturnalia, a brief excursion from his way of life." Nothing is more dull and anti-Bohemian than a teetotaler mentality, whether or not intoxicating substances are involved. "You never know what is enough unless you know what is more than enough," William Blake tells us. And he is right.

Think back on the best times you have had. Never once will you say: "Wasn't that a blast? Everybody behaved so moderately." Merriam-Webster defines moderation as "lessening the intensity." People willing to sit back and let others do the work of entertaining them don't deserve an invite to your party. And those who don't bring intensity to the way they live life—and this includes the way they approach their life's calling as well as the way they nap under a tree—are just not interested enough in the beauty and abundance around them to be interesting themselves. "There are several good protections against temptation, but the surest is coward-ice," Mark Twain said. It hardly sounds like he is in the anti-temptation camp. Step out! Risk embarrassment! Drink and eat life!

In the United States, our Puritan heritage often handcuffs our beautiful spirit. (Only in America could we believe a law such as prohibition would work.) Nothing drains the fun from the room like a prude. And what is a prude? A prude is someone who is afraid of what may be created by a group of uninhibited people. Few people are more honest than a drunk, whether drunk on wine, love, nature, or just plain joy. Abraham Lincoln understood this. "It has been my experience that folks who have no vices have no virtues," he said. And honesty is scary. Honesty disrupts. Honesty and appearance seldom meet, and probably wouldn't like each other if they did. Moderation is the hammer of prudishness, and prudishness restricts, inhibits, and denies. "Moderation has been called a virtue to limit the ambition of great men, and to console undistinguished people for their want of fortune and their lack of merit," Benjamin Disraeli rightly stated. Remember that the next time a prude looks at you in shock or disgust. It's his lack of merit that is speaking, wanting to drag you down to his level of grayness.

Don't give in. Ride the prudes' blushes like a surfer in a tsunami. Follow the sage advice of Mae West, who said, "People who are easily shocked should be shocked more often." Well said, Mae.

Before we get too far along, I need to be clear that I'm not promoting abusive behavior. This chapter follows the chapters on finding satisfactory work and rediscovering creativity for a reason. People who are unhappy in those areas tend to compensate by being excessive in other ways. If you do anything in excess in order to mask your problems and to numb your pain, whether it is drinking, eating, gambling, watching television or over-exercising, you are not Bohemian. That is the damaging, escapist behavior that I am railing against. Even the master of substance abuse, Keith Richards, knew when to *stop*. "That's where most people fuck up on drugs," he wrote. "It's the greed involved that never really affected me. People think once they've got this high, if they take some more, they're going to get a little higher. There's no such thing." Gluttony is not sexy. Stumbling around in a stupor is not enriching. "No matter how pleasurable a thing is, if you over-indulge in it, it ceases to give pleasure and gives pain instead," Yogi Paramahansa Yogananda writes. I'm not promoting excess; I'm promoting the unshackling of the spirit. Being present and being alive means understanding our limits. Some of us have had experiences or suffer from addictions that mean we should not drink. At all. Those of us in this category must find other ways to free our spirits from the shackles of moderation. But deprivation, instead of being a virtue, is often another excuse to avoid the fear of engaging life fully. Find your line and push it. Expand your circle. Don't be a wallflower in the dance hall of life.

Being consistently moderate is boring. Being good is important and fulfilling but balance is important: sometimes we need to be a little bad. "We're really good guys, but we can't be good every night," sang the band The Hold Steady. You don't need to be boorish or harmful to others. But when you get that little twinkle in your eye, when you get that little itch to shred your upstanding moral citizen costume, indulge a little. Scratch that itch. It keeps life interesting. It keeps you interesting. "Should we be completely rational beings without sins or weakness or misconduct, what

an insipid world that would be," says Lin Yutang. So don't be afraid to mis-
behave. It will be good for you. And if you embarrass yourself and look the
fool, at least you won't be dull. Just do it in a way that you don't surrender
your principles or hurt others. That would not be cool.

The key is, every once in a while, to just *let yourself go.* In his wonderful *Born to Run*, journalist Christopher McDougall documents the little
known Tarahumara tribe's amazing long distance running abilities.[xc] The
tribe lives in relative seclusion in the Copper Canyon region of North-
ern Mexico and McDougall became fascinated by their culture, which he
described as having "no corruption, obesity, drug addiction, wife-beating,
child abuse, high blood pressure, or carbon emissions." They were soft-
spoken, reticent, and seemed to lack the capacity to lie. However, every
once in a while, they will throw an elaborate party where they will drink *le-
chuguilla*, "a horrible homemade tequila brewed from rattlesnake corpses
and cactus sap." He described one party where these normally mild people
got so wasted "the wives began ripping each others' tops off in a bare-
breasted wrestling match, while a cackling old man circled around trying
to spear their butts with a corncob." Then the next day they woke up and
ran a two day race. I love it!

When you decide to do something, do it with abandon and without
shame or remorse. We have appetites—the wise man neither abuses nor
neglects them. Sometimes you will stumble, but more often you will soar.
And according to Michel De Montaigne, it goes against nature to ignore
our desire for pleasure.

> When I dance, I dance; when I sleep, I sleep; yes and when I walk alone in a beautiful
> orchard, if my thoughts have been concerned with extraneous incidents for some part of the time,
> for some other part I lead them back again to the walk, to the orchard, to the sweet-ness of this
> solitude, and to myself. Nature has in motherly fashion observed this principle, that the actions she
> has enjoined on us for our need should also give us pleasure; and she invites us to them not only
> through reason, but also through appetite. It is wrong to infringe her laws.

Hear that? Don't infringe on Nature's law. She can be vengeful. Go
live, indulge, and have some fun.

Love and Sex

I've been too fucking busy – or vice versa

**Dorothy Parker, in response to a letter from her editor
asking her to write stories while on her honeymoon.**

In the early 17th century, a group of pious people from England were sick and tired of someone else telling them what they could and couldn't do and decided to make a change: they would go to America where they could tell everyone else what they could and couldn't do. So they snubbed their nose at their philandering, head-chopping king and got on a boat and came to Plymouth.

In the new world, the elders of the Puritan community were determined to set up a spiritually pure, holy, Christian colony, where matters of the flesh would be left behind in decaying and decadent Britain. Despite strict laws and severe punishments, they failed. Why? They had misunderstood one very important fact:

Human beings really like sex.

It's true, and if that sentence makes you uncomfortable, you can thank the Puritans for the success they did achieve. They didn't break us of our love of sex, but they did succeed in making us feel guilty about it.

William Bradford (1597-1657) was an elder and historian of the early Plymouth colony, and he wrote of an outbreak in 1642 of "notorious sins" in the community, including "drunkenness, uncleanness, sodomy and buggery." The mortified elders blamed the Devil, of course, because he had "more power in these heathen lands" than in Christian Europe, where the Inquisition and Crusades had kept things nice with God.

The Devil may have made them do it, but people in Plymouth were gettin' it on. And it didn't matter whether it was with a partner (opposite sex or not), with themselves, or with animals. The town court records of September 7, 1642 record that "Thomas Graunger, late servant to Love Brewster of Duxborrow, was this Court indicted for buggery with a mare, a cowe, two goats, divers sheepe, two calves, and a turkey." That poor turkey. My image of the first Thanksgiving dinner shall be forever tainted. (*Excuse me, Squanto, but before I eat this, do you know with whom this turkey has been intimate?*) Don't fret, though. Justice was done and Graunger, a teenager, was put to death for failing to control his raging hormones. "A very sade spectacle it was; for first the mare, and then the cowe, and the rest of the lesser catle, were kild before his face, according to the law, Levit: 20.15 and then he himselfe was executed," sayeth the court records. I mean, *sure*, the *teenager* deserved to be executed . . . but the *cow?*[16]

And listen to the 1639 story of Mary Duxbury, a married Puritan woman, and her Native American lover, the plot of more than one future Harlequin romance:

> [She was charged] with dalliance divers tymes with Tinsin, an Indian, and after committing the act of uncleanesse wth him as by his owne confession by sevall interpters is made apparent, the Bench doth censure the said Mary to be whipt at a carts tayle through the townes streets, and to weare a badge upon her left sleeve during her aboad wthin this govnt; and if shee shalbe found wthout it abroad, then to be burned in the face wth a hott iron; and the said Tinsin, the Indian, to be well whipt wth a halter about his neck at the post, because it arose through the allurement & inticement of the said Mary, that hee was drawne thereunto.

As horrifically as Mary was treated, my heart goes out to Tinsin. There he was, living his own life with his own culture's morality, these new people show up and move onto his lands, and when he does what he's used to doing when a woman entices him, he is tied to a post by his neck and whipped. He had to wonder what the hell was going on. I'm wondering that myself.

Despite these sadistic punishments, Bradford and other historians of the day report numerous instances of carnal escapades, from public exposure, "chambering and wantonising" with sailors, premarital sex, and gen-

16 For the literal minded, the teenager did not deserve to be executed.

eral lewdness. They tried to buckle down on rape, though, and prohibited sex with a girl under the age of ten, *even though* "it be with her consent." Very righteous of them. I do know this: if *Desperate Plymouth Housewives* becomes a television show, I'm tuning in.

Puritans, and our contemporaries who still subscribe to their view, mistake propriety and deprivation for goodness. Their approach values form more than substance. They believed pleasure, desire, lust and debauchery can't share space with love, compassion and spirituality in the heart of a man. (In 1645 the Puritans who stayed in England and eventually gained power went as far as to ban Christmas. Too much merry making.) These complex feelings and character traits can and do share space within each of us, of course. Oscar Schindler, the hero who saved hundreds of Jews from the Nazis, was a notorious alcoholic and womanizer. Winston Churchill, the rock of England who led the Brits to victory in WWII, was a heavy drinker, smoker and nap indulger. Hitler, the teetotaling vegetarian puppy lover, was, well, Hitler. Repressing our carnality can be dangerous because if not expressed, our desires tend to leak out in creepy perversions, like voting for Rick Santorum.

If the word "Puritan" has an antonym, it is "Bohemian." A good way to define what Bohemian love *is* would be by describing what it *is not*, and that is what was expected in good William Bradford's New England. Bohemians have been rebelling against such false piety for centuries.

But what does it mean to be a Bohemian in love? The stereotype certainly calls forth images of debauchery and loosened marital boundaries. We think of Toulouse-Lautrec loving one of many prostitutes in Montmartre or Gauguin and his scantily clad Tahitian beauties. "For us Spaniards, it's Mass in the morning, the bullfight in the afternoon, the brothel in the evening," Picasso said. Vanessa and Clive Bell, the founding members of the Bloomsbury Group, had an open marriage and both took different lovers during their lives. (Vanessa's sister, the future Virginia Woolf, had an open and ongoing flirtation with Clive that lasted for years. In May 1908 he wrote in one of his letters to Virginia, "I wished for nothing in the world but to kiss you.") Bohemian morality, is, well, *different* than that of the bourgeoisie. After returning to the Bloomsbury Group following an extended absence, Leonard Woolf wrote, "They produce a sense—often unconscious—of intimacy and freedom, and so break down barriers to thought and feeling. It was this feeling of greater intimacy and feeling, of the sweeping away of formalities and barriers, which I found so new and so exhilarating in 1911."[xci] They were excited, ready to question and challenge conventional morality and relations among couples. They were adventurous.

In the Bohemian world, convention carries little value. Love, pleasure and experience are what the Bohemian seeks. But the idea of casting all other matters aside in the name of love was not created by the Bohemians; that idea has been around since the serpent seduced Eve in the Garden. Something in us wants the kind of love that can't be stopped or restrained, no matter the costs. "Let the lover be disgraceful, crazy, absentminded," Rumi wrote. "Someone sober will worry about events going badly. Let the lover be."

Alas, this doesn't come without consequences. The problem with putting experience, pleasure and self-gratification above all other considerations is that the people you love get hurt. Anaïs Nin didn't want her diaries published until after her husband's death because she didn't want him to know about her many lovers. Despite her secrecy, her affair with Henry Miller put tremendous strain on her marriage and pushed her into therapy. There are people who can make open relationships work, but they are rare. Inevitably, one partner will seem to be getting more love than the other, and then the ugly emotions—anger, jealousy, neediness—raise their heads. Bohemians are no exception. In her memoir of Generation X Bohemian life, *Weird Like Us*, Ann Powers discusses the concept that Bohemians, by outwardly rejecting the moral codes of conventional society, are still not prone to transcend them. In describing the early years of modern Bohemian life, she writes:

> To learn the history of the Left Bank or Greenwich Village is to discover an endless string of husbands taking advantage of the labor of their wives, keeping mistresses on the side, leaving

their children with no emotional support, and ultimately claiming that the women who pampered them were as square as the parents they rejected.

That isn't unconventionality; that's simply conventional bad behavior. And how did the Bloomsbury Group's experiments with love work out? Not as they hoped. "Perhaps deliberately, Virginia was driving a wedge between herself and Vanessa, punishing her sister for changing their relationship by marrying Clive," Peter Stansky wrote.[xcii] Despite being married to Vanessa, Clive didn't like the idea of Virginia being with another man and worried that she might marry Lytton Strachey, despite Strachey being homosexual. Vanessa had her limits as well. "Vanessa may have never completely forgiven Virginia for [the flirtation with Clive], and it may have helped prepare the way for a change in the nature of Clive and Vanessa's intimacy," Stansky wrote. More like soap opera melodrama than brave new world.

I'm all for unconventional love, but I must confess I am a romantic and a believer that unconventional love within a relationship with one person—the person one loves—is the way to true Bohemian love. In describing her early years of communal living in San Francisco, Powers admits, with a few notable exceptions, that contemporary Bohemians' ability to be happy outside of a committed relationship with one person is as limited as it has ever been. "The primacy of the couple remains so strong in our society that even those who consciously strive to challenge it usually fail. David [my partner] and I certainly did."

However, notable and admirable exceptions exist. I met Annette[17] at a conference and when I told her about my Bohemian writing project, she opened up with her own story. In her early twenties she fell in love and married a man twenty years her senior. Two years into the marriage, he was struck with Parkinson's disease and his health deteriorated quickly. Due to his condition, they were no longer able to have sex. She loved him, cared for him and stayed married. Twenty years later, she realized she could no longer live without that aspect of her life. Instead of leaving him she opened

---

17 Not her real name.

up to him and explained her longings and her needs. He understood. They are still married and she now has a boyfriend in which she expresses the part of her life she can't with her husband. She showed great love to remain devoted and caring to her husband for a lifetime. It was brave of her to be open and truthful to him about her needs. It was loving and brave of him to overcome potential jealousy and resentments to let her experience what she needed.

An unusual circumstance for sure. And I'm sure some outsiders would still judge them harshly, but I honor them for their choices. Most of us would not be able to maintain such a balance in a relationship. But committing to one person is no excuse for settling. The anti-moderation rule applies here also: love fully, or get out. And that means putting yourself at risk. "There are no guarantees but if you don't love you're a coward," Jim Harrison wrote. Be brave enough to be unconventional with the one you love. Sex advice columnist Dan Savage advises lovers to be "GGG"— good, giving, and game—with their partners, which means taking the time to learn the art of love and what your lover appreciates as well as having an open mind and a willingness to explore. Many people lose interest not because of their partner, but due to their own inhibitions and lack of imagination. Treat love as art, as sex therapist Esther Perel described in an interview with *The Idler* magazine:

> The people who have the spark are the people who know how to invite ceremony, ritual, playfulness—inside their own home. And that's how they create their own sexual space, fantasy space . . . [The people who don't] imagine that they can finish the dishes, turn off the television, go upstairs and just get going! Without any ritual or ceremony, nothing to anticipate. In order to want sex, it needs to be sex worth wanting.[xciii]

When I first began working as an attorney and handled divorce cases, I was miserable. I worked with people at their lowest ebb; people who were heartbroken, bitter, angry and destructive. I watched them destroy their lives for the sole purpose of hurting their partner, the person that at one time they believed they loved more than any other. I watched children being used as pawns. With my temperament, I knew I would not be able to distance myself from my clients and their pain enough to thrive or even endure that kind of work and I stopped doing it very quickly. When I went through my own divorce, I experienced the pain of separation and the resulting toll on my and my wife's rationality and emotional stability. Like many, we married young, before we truly understood ourselves and who we were and wanted to be in this life. Our respective goals, wants and needs diverged more and more as time went on. Discovering and accepting this was slow and devastating to both of us, and the wounds ran deep for a long time. Years later, I am able to look back and see the value of the relationship. I am grateful that it existed and grateful that it ended.

I firmly believe in working through problems. As the writer Ed Davis says, "A career, or a marriage, for that matter, is not to live happily ever after. The relationship exists to teach you who you are." Many people destroy valuable relationships because they are unable or unwilling to suffer the pain of growth required throughout inevitable stages of development and change. But I equally believe that when the relationship is over—truly over, not just challenged—the Bohemian is willing to move on, to let go and to forgive, no matter how hard. I see many relationships that from the outside look happy but are secretly loveless, the couple staying together because they fear being alone or losing financial security or status. Some are stuck in pure stasis. It's sad to witness, and it's a half-life.

Wise Bohemians know not to rely on someone else to make them happy. They explore and experience and create to find their own happiness, and if they have someone to love along the way, all the better. "As long as you are looking to another—whether it's a parent, a child, a friend, a spouse, a guru or anyone—to fill that within you which is hurt, to put back together that within you is broken, you will never be able to experience true love," teaches Pujya Swami Chidanand Saraswatiji. Tom Robbins agrees.

> When we're incomplete, we're always searching for somebody to complete us. When, after a few years or a few months of a relationship, we find that we're still unfulfilled, we blame our partners and take up with somebody more promising. This can go on and on–series polygamy–until we admit that while a partner can add sweet dimensions to our lives, we, each of us, are responsible for our own fulfillment. Nobody else can provide it for us, and to believe otherwise is

to delude ourselves dangerously and to program for eventual failure every relationship we enter.[xciv]

I've certainly been guilty of what Robbins is describing. In past love affairs, I have expected my partner to complete me and make me happy. This expectation set up an inevitable fear of losing that person and along with her my happiness. And this fear will poison a relationship and ultimately kill it off. I believe this is a mistake many of us make in our youth. Most of us want to be in a love relationship with someone else, but we shouldn't look to that person to make us happy. Only you can make you happy. Create a space of love within yourself and it will radiate outward to all things. Invite your lover to step into that warm space. And allow her to step back out when she needs to. If you do this freely, she will return. If she doesn't you've created a place that someone else will. As with all things, we succeed some times more than others. We must accept that insecurity and jealousy and loneliness are part of relationships, too. But with open, loving hearts, we can learn from these feelings, let them go and move on.

Bohemians are romantics; Bohemians are lovers. But they are seekers and creators first. Be who you are and follow your path. If you are passionate about your life, lovers will be drawn to you. And you can write your own unconventional love story.

Food and Drink

Alcohol beats the shit out of the Shroud of Turin as a miracle.

Jim Harrison

A sunny day in the park, a bottle of wine, and a picnic basket filled with fruit, cheeses, and bread. Lighted candles, snow falling outside the window, and a long table of delicacies to be shared with delightful friends. Lunch with colleagues, a scandalous martini, and getting back to the office an hour late. Dicing, stirring, smelling, and tasting the spoon handed to you by your lover in the kitchen. The potluck around a campfire. Ah, the joy of food, of the meal, of the toast, of communion with our brethren, where the only sin is the drive-through, the rushed, the wasted moment! Let us raise our glasses and not leave the table for hours, for we are Bohemians and have much to savor and many stories to tell. We never indulge unless we want to, and we often want to. Here's to the uncorked bottle and the warm oven!

Healthy eating is important, and because of the value Bohemians put on the sensual pleasure of food, I believe they eat better than most. Viewing food as fuel, something that needs to be measured, counted, powdered and pilled—how very bourgeois! Food is life, and the meal is the celebration of this life. Give it the time, the preparation, the appreciation it deserves. Shame on us for bringing the all-you-can-eat buffet and high fructose corn syrup into the world. Toss aside your soda and tap your homebrew!

But let us not *seek* happiness by eating and drinking with our friends, but to *express* the happiness we feel in their presence, in our world, in the beautiful moment, so sayeth the wise Lin Yutang:

There is a proper time and place for getting drunk. One should get drunk before flowers in

168

the daytime, in order to assimilate their light and color; and one should get drunk in the snow in the nighttime, in order to clear his thoughts. A man getting drunk when happy at success should sing, in order to harmonize the spirit; and a man getting drunk at a farewell party should strike a musical tone, in order to strengthen his spirit . . . There are proper ways of drinking in respect of mood and scenery, and to violate these rules is to miss the pleasure of drinking.

Yutang advises using alcohol to enhance experience, not to obliterate reality. Here is Basil describing Zorba enjoying his liquor: "He drank his rum in little sips, keeping it a long time in his mouth to get the taste, then letting it slip slowly down and warm his insides." That is not moderation; that is appreciation. That is joy. I've always associated drinking with celebration and agree with the Latin proverb that "it is well to remember that there are five reasons for drinking: the arrival of a friend, one's present or future thirst, the excellence of the wine, or any other reason." Tom Robbins praises tequila's power to sever the chains of respectability. Having discovered good tequila in the company of the fun-loving Mexican people, I can agree with Robbins' luscious description:

Now tequila may be the favoured beverage of outlaws but that doesn't mean it gives them preferential treatment. In fact, tequila probably has betrayed as many outlaws as has the central nervous system and dissatisfied wives. Tequila, scorpion honey, harsh dew of the doglands, essence of Aztec, crema de cacti; tequila, oily and thermal like the sun in solution; tequila, liquid geometry of passion; Tequila, the buzzard god who copulates in midair with the ascending souls of dying virgins; tequila, firebug in the house of good taste; O tequila, savage water of sorcery, what confusion and mischief your sly, rebellious drops do generate![xcv]

Any liquid that can inspire that description is okay in my book. There are many ways to free our spirit, most of them better than alcohol. But alcohol *is* pretty good. Here is Tom Hodgkinson describing the first drink at happy hour:

It marks the end of the working day, when you put worldly cares to one side and embrace good cheer and company. It is when the soul opens and we are seized by the need to chat. We are liberated. After spending the day either living in the past (regrets, reports) or the future (anxieties, PowerPoint presentations), the first drink of the day brings us into the present moment: we become Buddhists.

A bit tongue and cheek, perhaps, but holding a kernel of truth. I'm not promoting alcohol—it certainly doesn't need my help to find an eager audience. But I'm encouraging you, as a Bohemian, if you choose to indulge to find the *art* in alcohol. Alcohol doesn't inspire creativity—that's a myth that we'd do well to dismiss. More often, alcohol and drugs impede the creative process, temporarily or permanently. We have lost years of art from talented people who have died young from their vices. And don't use alcohol or food—or any substance or activity for that matter—to escape difficult times or emotional pain. Being Bohemian is being able to be in touch with all experiences, good and bad. But by all means, if you can find the joy in it, enjoy it. "Contemplating our food for a few seconds before eating in mindfulness can bring us much happiness," Thich Nhat Hanh writes. I think Zorba, drinking his rum earlier, was doing it in a mindful way, too. Find the beauty in a glass of wine, a lively table, and good talk. Share the joy of trading descriptions of tequila with Tom Robbins. Drape yourself in a cloak of romantic mystique by sharing a glass of Absinthe with a beautiful woman in a dark pub in Prague. Let the champagne bubbles roll up your spine as you spin your partner on the dance floor. Learn to *savor.*

And then know when to stop. And for some of us, that can mean forever. And if not forever, it's wise to occasionally go through a period of temperance to make sure you still can. You certainly don't *need* to drink to be Bohemian.

When the experience starts to become cloudy, dull or uninspiring, cork the bottle, roll over in the grass, and listen to your lover read you poetry. And if you get sleepy, fall into dreamy bliss in her lap, remembering it will be her turn next time.

Music and Dance

They danced down the streets like dingledodies, and I shambled after as I've been doing all my life after people who interest me, because the only people for me are the mad ones, the ones who are mad to live, mad to talk, mad to be saved, desirous of everything at the same time, the ones that never yawn or say a commonplace thing, but burn, burn, burn . . .

Jack Kerouac

Do you know what a dingledodie is? I don't.[18] But I'm going to dance like one before I die. I haven't got there yet (still too much Midwestern shyness to burn through) but I'm getting close. What is it about dance? Well, let's start with the freeing nature of it. It allows us to be in our bodies—with the possible exception of sex—like no other form of expression. "There is a bit of insanity in dancing that does everybody a great deal of good," said poet Edwin Denby. Will we look ridiculous? Perhaps. But the metaphysical question you must ask is: who gives a shit? A Japanese proverb wisely advises that we're fools whether we dance or not, so we might as well dance. Do it alone if your self-consciousness requires, but be in your body. In the West many of us have cut ourselves off from the wisdom our bodies have to offer us. The brain becomes Captain Kirk, sitting in the cockpit, and the body the Starship Enterprise, no more than a big machine to move our mind from place to place. Not so, my friends. Give yourself over to your body from time to time, and that means to give yourself over to free-expressing movement. What I'm describing is much different than working out or running, which certainly have their place. Dancing is exercise, too, but that's merely a side benefit. "Dance is the hidden language of the soul," said Martha Graham. Learn that language. Feel your body commune with itself and its environment, without your mind constantly fighting for control.

---

18 The consensus is Kerouac made up the word "dingledodie."

Dayton native Sheri "Sparkle" Williams is a star dancer with the Dayton Contemporary Dance Company. At the time of writing she was forty-eight years old (she doesn't look a day over thirty-five) and has been dancing with the company for *thirty-eight years*. As with others interviewed, I wanted to explore with her how to remain true to your passion while making ends meet and how to survive the tough times when money is short or passions wane. I knew right away that my approach wasn't going to work—she is so relentlessly positive that it was impossible to talk of the downside of anything with her. The only complaint I could draw from her was that the cold makes it more difficult to practice in winter. She may be the most authentically upbeat person I have ever met.

Since she was discovered at age eleven by the director of the dance company, she has performed in forty-eight states and on five continents. She has danced on Broadway and in thousand-year-old Roman theaters. She has won the Bessie Award, contemporary dance's version of the Oscar.

She's the perfect example of someone who was able to earn enough from her passion to live well without needing to divert her energy to other things to make ends meet, and she's done it for a lifetime. It is difficult for her to understand people who live otherwise. "I look around and I see all these people who do things that they just don't like," she says. "I hate hearing that, because I so enjoy what I do. Do I want to get up every morning and come here? No. Sometimes I don't want to. But I love it."

Like anything worth doing, dancing professionally is hard work requiring hours of daily practice and training. Much of her success and happiness she attributes to the Dayton Contemporary Dance Company. Despite the company being recognized around the world and attracting dancers from everywhere, being located in the Midwest away from the pretensions and pressures that sometimes face similar dance companies on the coasts allows an atmosphere of ease and community to go along with the discipline. "They work you hard, not to beat you down, but to bring out your best," she says. And her experience has taught her to strive for perfection while being able to laugh off the inevitable faults and mistakes that come with being human. "People are so tense about making a mistake," she says. "I'm not saying it's all right to mess up, but it happens. We are not machines. Recognize it and move on. Be able to laugh at it." She and her compatriots often dance with injuries and through pain. One time she performed with a concussion. But for her, dance has not been the cause of pain, but the healer of it.

In a five-year period, her mother, her father and her sister died. Her mother passed away in her arms, and Sheri still chose to travel with the troupe rather than drop out of a performance. Her sister died at forty-four, leaving three minor children whom Sheri raised. Following hip replacement surgery, her father moved in as well. He suffered a heart attack and died in her house. He died at 8:00 in the morning and at 8:00 p.m. she was performing. She says if she had stopped, she would have sunk with grief. Dance kept her going.

I believe her happy disposition has much to do with her choice of artistic expression. Dance, more than any other artistic endeavor, provides us near instant, euphoric joy. Watching a recent performance by DCDC, I believe Sheri knows what Josephine Baker meant when she said, " I became crazed by the music . . . even my teeth and eyes burned with fever. Each time I leaped I seemed to touch the sky and when I regained earth it seemed to be mine alone." And one doesn't need be as talented as Sheri or Josephine. We can move, shake and twist our awkward, amateur bodies and experience just as much.

Sheri "Sparkle" Williams performing with the Dayton Contemporary Dance Company. Photograph by Scott Robbins.

Dancing does more than make us happy, though. It preserves our mind. A *New England Journal of Medicine* study found that dancing frequently reduced the risk of incurring a mentally degenerative disease by 76%.[xcvi] To illustrate how impressive this is, doing crossword puzzles only scored a 47% and reading 35%, while golfing, biking, and swimming all scored a whopping 0%.

Even the *observance* of dance can have miraculous effects. At the age of thirty-one, author Paul Auster was enduring the darkest time of his life. His first marriage had ended, he was the father of a one-year-old son and had no job or money to support him, and was barely surviving as a freelance translator and writer of critical essays for magazines such as *Harper's*. He was suffering from severe writer's block and began doubting that he would ever write again. Such was his state of mind when a friend invited him to a rehearsal for a new dance performance in New York City. When the dancers began he was surprised there was no musical accompaniment, but he soon became transfixed with the dancers' movement through the silence. Watching this shook his moorings. He wrote:

> Something began to open up inside you, you found yourself falling through the rift between world and word, the chasm that divides human life from our capacity to understand or express the truth of human life, and for reasons that still confound you, this sudden fall through the empty, unbounded air filled you with a sensation of freedom and happiness, and by the time the performance was over, you were no longer blocked.[xcvii]

Auster went home and began writing. And the beauty of the dance was the trigger that released him from his depression and blocked creativity. Thirty years and twenty-eight books later, he is still going.

Our dancing need not be limited to the studio, the nightclub, or the wedding reception. Unscheduled, solitary dance can be the most satisfying and freeing of all. "Dance, even if you have nowhere to do it but your living room," said Kurt Vonnegut. Do what Springsteen sings: turn off the lights and dance in the dark. This form of dancing is freeing because it is not about structure, it is not about courting the opposite sex and it is not about exhibition or overcoming shyness. It is about reintroducing your soul to your body. Make a soundtrack, clear the floor, close the curtains, and move. Start slowly. Feel ridiculous and embarrassed if that is how you feel. It will subside. As you begin to ease into the flow of your own movement, your muscles will relax and your abusing ego will lose its influence. You will be present in the moment and in your body and soon you will be lost in the music's rhythm. Close your eyes and spin like you did as a child. Play some tribal percussion music and rediscover your primal side. Your suit and tie or high heels will still be there afterward. If the music is loud enough—and yes, it should be loud—you won't scare the neighbors with your primal YAWLP that comes from the depth of your belly when you reach that place of freedom and bliss that unfettered dance brings.

Dancing rids us of stress and can be a method of meditation. The Yogi Osho suggests we engage in *Kundalini* or "active meditation" at the end of a workday. He advises to shake "your rock-like being to its very foundation such that it becomes liquid, fluid, such that it melts, flows." Kundalini involves four steps: fifteen minutes of shaking to loosen the body, fifteen minutes of free dance, fifteen minutes of being still, either sitting or standing, observing what is happening inside and outside of you, and fifteen minutes of lying still. I tried this recently and it is wonderfully refreshing and stress-relieving. Rapturous, even. Even though I was alone I was shy doing this at first, and I'm sure at times I looked as silly as a shaved monkey, but as Bono said, "I reserve the right to look ridiculous." I felt great during and afterward. And it was fun. So go close the curtains, crank up the music, and get moving.

Reading

Good friends, good books and a sleepy conscience: this is the ideal life.

Mark Twain

A winter's day, a chair by the fireplace, a glass of wine. In the coffee shop on the corner of a busy street. In a bar, waiting for a friend. In the hammock, the checkout line, the bus stop. In bed before falling asleep or upon waking the next morning. On the beach and on the plane. Under the covers while your parents think you are sleeping. The pleasure of a good book: few gifts are more giving.

Many Bohemians are novelists, poets, playwrights and screenwriters for a reason: there is something magical about story. A poem can touch us like the hand of a lover; a novel gives us an alternate life. Storytelling connects us with our humanity and allows us to experience empathy in an unparalleled way. Michael Ondaatje, writing in *The English Patient*, described this experience beautifully when his character Sara picks a book off the shelf in the abandoned villa in which she is living and waiting for WWII to end: "She entered the story knowing she would emerge from it feeling she had been immersed in the lives of others, in plots that stretched back twenty years, her body full of sentences and moments, as if awakening from sleep with a heaviness caused by unremembered dreams." This state of dreamy escape is what Lin Yutang meant when he said that when reading, "The reader is always carried away into a world of thought and reflection . . . the man who has not the habit of reading is imprisoned in his immediate world, in respect to time and space."

Oh how I pity those who don't know the joy of getting lost in a beautiful story! I think of Miles in the film *Sideways*[xcviii] when he tells his friend's future father-in-law that he has written a novel. The father-in-law responds that he only reads nonfiction because "there is so much to know about this world. I think reading something somebody just invented is a waste of time."

"That's an interesting perspective," Miles politely responds. The father-in-law is making the fatal flaw of confusing actuality with reality. The fact the stories are "made up" does not limit the underlying truth a great author can convey, but more often, the vehicle of story enhances our ability to appreciate and be moved by its truth. The novelist and poet Alice Walker was so moved by the description of child abuse in *Jane Eyre* that she fully supports an orphanage in Africa. Good fiction does just that—it touches our soul and it feeds our sense of compassion. It inspires us to act.

Great novels have changed my life and shaped my character in priceless ways. J.D. Salinger made me feel alive and not alone when an early adolescent, and then made me feel a sad, distanced empathy for him when I reread *Catcher In The Rye* as an adult. *To Kill A Mockingbird*'s Atticus Finch taught me gentility, honor, and bravery more than any knight or soldier could have. Kerouac helped me understand my longing to escape the confines of my life in my late teens, and showed me a way to do it. Nick Hornby helped me through my morose and relationship-challenged thirties. Milan Kundera helped me understand Communism and the human condition in a way my history classes never did. My father and I wouldn't have had as much fun searching for arrowheads in the forest and streams of his parents' farm in Kentucky if he hadn't encouraged me to read *The Last of the Mohicans*. The list goes on and on. But perhaps most importantly, *Babbitt* and *Revolutionary Road* brought home truths about my own tendency to conform and settle that rattled my cage and woke me up. I knew I had to make big changes in my life to avoid big regrets.

Poetry is meditation, it is prayer, it is a time to pause, to reflect, to enliven the senses. I try to start my mornings with a poem from Rumi, Rilke, Alice Walker and a few others. These artists offer a gift, a substance to guide and carry me through the day more so than any news program. The depth of feeling conveyed in a mere nine lines by Raymond Carver in his poem *Rain* is testament to the power of poetry. I read it, and I think, *I know, Ray. I know.* Do not deny yourself this gift, my friends.

Books are old and loyal friends, waiting patiently on my bookshelves to drop into a hammock with me on an idle day. I met a man at a bar who, when hearing I like to write, bragged (yes, *bragged*) that he hadn't read a book since high school. He pointed out the window to his Ferrari, which I complimented. I left feeling the richer of the two. Money, or lack thereof, isn't a problem when it comes to the joy of reading. Thank Ben Franklin for coming up with the idea of public libraries.

Reading is good for your health, too. "Bibliotherapy" is a treatment in which therapists or doctors prescribe reading, typically classic or literary fiction, to alleviate symptoms and to help a patient heal by going through three stages: identification, catharsis, and insight. *Romeo and Juliet* is commonly used for troubled teens because the protagonists are their contemporaries and their problems relatable. One study even found that reading fiction activated brain activity that protected smelter workers from brain damage following lead poisoning.[xcix] According to the study, reading contributes to 'cognitive reserve,' which is the brain's ability to protect itself from physical damage.

Studies also showed that people suffering from depression who couldn't or wouldn't seek traditional counseling but read regularly had a higher success rate of recovery than those who didn't read. Based on my own experience, this finding is not surprising. When depressed, lonely, sad or grieving, it helps to read about people experiencing these same feelings. You learn from how they react, the choices they make and the consequences that follow. You are reminded that you are not alone in what you feel and that you are part of the vast human experience. That is comforting. Poems In The Waiting Room, a charity program based in the United Kingdom, offers short collections of poems to patients to read while waiting to enter surgery. These studies and efforts may be recent, but the conclusions are not new. The ancient Greeks posted signs above the door of libraries calling them "The healing place of the soul."

"We should read to give our souls a chance to luxuriate," says Henry Miller. Reading the daily newspaper is fine, but that's not what he means. Seek enrichment, not information. It's depth of feeling you want. It's connection with yourself and all that is. "Reading well is one of the great pleasures that solitude can afford you," writes Harold Bloom. Grab a good book. Sit by your fireplace or head to the coffee shop. Turn the page and explore a new world, a different time, and a life other than your own. Yours may never be the same.

Travel

Daddy said, son, you better see the world
I wouldn't blame you if you wanted to leave

"Every Picture Tells a Story," by Rod Stewart

In May of my twenty-second year, I stepped off a plane at the Charles De Gaulle Airport in Paris, the first time I had traveled abroad. Alone, no one meeting me at the gate, no hotel arrangements, and no plans until my study abroad classes started two weeks later. I was fearful, proud, and exhilarated. For people who grew up traveling, this experience may seem almost passé, hardly warranting me the title Brave Adventurer. But my previous travel experiences were limited to visiting extended family a few states away and enjoying long weekends at American cities for soccer tournaments. My family didn't have the resources for exotic travel, but I lived vicariously through the stories my father told me of his travels through Europe while stationed in Germany in his Army days. He and his buddies would take off on furlough, hop a train to anywhere and have experiences that would last a lifetime. Those stories, along with the adventure novels I devoured growing up, had planted the travel bug deep within me. I could care less about the classes in international business and antitrust law I would be taking, but I was smitten with Angelica from Austria, and that's the program that got me the student loan to get there.

Stepping off that train into the unknown (unknown to me, and when it comes to life changing experiences, that's what matters) did not disappoint. When I returned home, I would not be the same person who landed that day. I met people who were unlike any I had known before, but had more in common with me than most people that I'd grown up with my entire life. I had food that I didn't know existed and developed a love of wine, trains and cafés. I made deep friendships that will last a lifetime. I had mugs of beer on mountain peaks in the Alps and in underground pubs. I discovered nude beaches aren't really the titillating experience I thought they'd be (anyone you would want to see naked is clothed and everyone you wouldn't want to see is strutting in the buff). A Czech Republic train conductor demanded a bribe before he would stamp my ticket and let me off the train. I ran out of money. I had moments of joy, confusion and lone-liness. Occasionally I had the sneaky feeling that someone was insulting me in his own language. I loved every minute of it. I had much to see and learn, but a life-long traveler had been born. And I had many Bohemians to inspire me.

In *Garrets and Pretenders*, Albert Parry documents the life of the artist George "Pops" Hart, a Bohemian traveler worthy of respect. In 1900 Hart traveled the Mississippi by steamer to New Orleans. From there he hopped on a ship to Naples, stayed for a while, and then moved on to Egypt, where "he bummed up the Nile river . . . lived with Arabs in their city slums and desert tents, and painted on a derelict barge which was his studio," wrote Parry. He returned to America and lived in San Francisco for a brief time before traveling to Tahiti and then Samoa, where he "was be-trothed to the daughter of a native chief, drank and danced with his would-be relatives, but escaped when the business grew too serious and prosaic." He built a shack in Honolulu, where much "dancing, singing, guitar- and ukulele-playing" occurred. From there it was Cuba, then Haiti, then Ice-land, and finally Mexico, "where he fell in love with a native girl and tried to make her primitive while she wanted the clothes from Paris and the high-heel shoes from New York."

How did he do this? He was a painter, and at each place he found work as an itinerant sign painter. He didn't need much except for the free-dom to explore the world and the limited means it took for him to do it. He was not independently wealthy; he had no trust fund; he had not won the lottery. (When he arrived in Tahiti, he had only five dollars in his pocket.) He had no itinerary, travel agents, or hotels booked months in advance. But he saw the world and lived a life that leaves me gasping in its breadth and beauty. Many of us never cross our border because we think we can't afford it or are afraid of what might happen to us on the other side. Bravo, Pops Hart.

But that was two hundred years ago, you might argue. That's not possible in the modern world. Today, travel is too expensive. Looking at the prices in *Condé Nast* magazine, one might agree. But tell that to Chris Guillebeau, who, though still in his thirties (and not a trustfunder, by the way) has traveled to all 193 countries that are members of the United Nations. I recommend you check out his blog at ChrisGuillebeau.com and his book, *The Art of Non-conformity,* for more of his story and for tips on travel and other unconventional living and working advice. His stories, from running marathons in Cuba to interviewing aid workers in Sudan, paradoxically make the world feel bigger and smaller at the same time. Another great source for traveling without breaking the bank is Daytonian Scott Ford's packabagandgo.com. On a trip, Scott gave up his seat on an overbooked flight for a free-flight voucher, and by continuing to do this each subsequent flight, he took fifty-two trips in fifty-two weeks and racked up one million frequent flier miles, *all for free.* (Another perk was free hotels along the way.) Creativity is not limited to screenplays and oil canvases. Scott has turned inexpensive travel into an art form.

Perhaps not surprisingly, another reason many refrain from traveling is fear. I recently spent three weeks traveling with a friend through Peru. When I told others about my upcoming trip, the most common concern was the risk of being away from work so long. "Are you worried about losing clients?" I was repeatedly asked. The answer is no. Losing clients is a risk, I suppose, but not a troublesome one. I'm sure I've lost out on opportunities to make money because I wasn't available, but that opens up an opportunity for someone else and as long as I maintain the income stream to meet my needs, the tradeoff is worth it. Not all of us have the same level of flexibility, but within our different schedules, we can, and must, make room for stepping away from our routine. My brother is a teacher and cannot jump on a plane on a whim, but must wait for the scheduled breaks the school system provides. But those breaks are ample and it is up to him to take advantage of them. Many people have other restrictions to overcome, such as young children, but nothing is impossible. Just ask the writers of the blog *Soultravelers3.com*, a mother, father and five-year-old daughter who took a year off to travel around the world. They decided they wanted the enriching experience of international extended travel and they figured out a way to make it happen. Read their blog to find out more.

We must remember the adage of work to live, not live to work. The average American receives one week of vacation per year and often *doesn't use it*. If we do use our vacation time, we often stay at home. If we go somewhere, it's to a place that we've already been and find unintimidating. Back to Disneyland again.

Other fear-based questions I was asked when discussing my Peru trip: Aren't you afraid of terrorists? Being kidnapped? Getting robbed? Is the government stable? Is the water safe? Sigh. Yes, many others expressed excitement and encouragement, but I am continually surprised at the number of fears and excuses people have for not stepping outside their front door.

Bohemians are travelers, not tourists. Bohemians seek to discover new cultures, not expect to find home wherever they go. Stepping away from what is known and comfortable is a wonderful way to discover new things about ourselves and to open up channels of creativity and ways of thinking that would not be possible otherwise. Growing up on the doctrine that "the United States is the greatest country in the world," I remember how shocked I was in my early twenties when I went on that first European trip and met people who, although they liked Americans, did not want to trade places. They liked what their country had to offer better. And for some things, (method of payment for education and healthcare, value of time away from work, less prudish sexual attitudes) I agreed with them. I love my country and will forever remain an American wherever I am, but my prospective was broadened.

My subsequent traveling experiences have also shifted and altered who I am. We tend to become static and rigid when confined to the same space, place, and people for too long. We tend to form opinions about others and the world that aren't true. Most Americans I know who dislike the French have never been to France or met a French person. I can't think of one stereotype I had of a culture that didn't dissolve after interacting with its people, but this one more than most. When I arrived at the airport on that first trip abroad when I was twenty-two, a very helpful travel assistant found me a cheap room in the Left Bank, and when on the train I asked a tired businessman on his way home from work what stop I needed to take for my hotel, he got off at the stop with me and walked me to the hotel because he said it was difficult to find. When we got there, he shook my hand and walked the three blocks through the winding streets back to wait for the next train. Later that week, I was walking through the city with Katie, an Australian I had met, and we stopped outside a house where a woman was working in her garden to ask if we could fill our empty water bottles at her garden faucet. The woman shook her head no, and told us to wait. She stepped inside and returned with two bottles of Evian for us.

When I traveled with my friend Arturo to his hometown of Santa Anna, Mexico for the town's annual festival, the locals I met bent over backward to make me feel welcome, well fed, and entertained. At one point an old man, stooped, fragile, but looking proud in his cowboy hat and bolo tie, approached me, shook my hand, and spoke to me in Spanish. Arturo told me he was thanking me for all that my country had done for his family. I was deeply touched. Disagreeable people can be found everywhere, but my positive experiences shattered my expectations.

And you don't have to travel to expensive or exotic places to experience the joys that travel has to offer. "The philosophy of travel as consisting of the capacity to see things, which abolishes the distinction between travel to a distant country and going about the fields of an afternoon," says Lin Yutang. After experiencing a devastating divorce and losing his job, William Least Heat-Moon bought a van, packed it with food and travel gear, and took off across the United States with $454 to his name. His idea was to go wherever the road took him, to meet new people, and to just be open to what may happen. "A man who couldn't make things go right could at least go," he wrote. "He could quit trying to get out of the way of life and live the real jeopardy of circumstance." He documented his journey in his book *Blue Highway,*[c] a bestseller that was translated into thirty-nine different languages and is still popular thirty years after publication.

As with Least Heat-Moon, the need to travel often follows an upheaval in life. Other times it comes from the sense that one's life is stuck. You need new experiences to open the flow of energy and rediscover your passion and creativity again. The Australian Aborigines have a tradition of going on a "walkabout," which Merriam-Webster's Dictionary describes as "a short period of wandering . . . as an occasional interruption of work . . . making a ritual journey." We all need a walkabout from time to time. We don't grow when locked in routine for too long. And to take a journey, particularly one involving several weeks or a month, is an unconventional act in our modern culture. I believe from time to time we all get that faraway look in our eyes and long to be a nomad, a gypsy, a wanderer. It pays to acknowledge and feed that part of our souls.

And being a traveler has yet another gift to offer us: the return home. The return to our own pillow and favorite coffee cup. To our books, pets, friends and neighbors. To our loved ones. Absence does make the heart grow fonder. Curl up in your favorite chair with your journals and photographs and relish the comforts of home and dream of your next adventure.

Make travel a priority, my Bohemian friends. And not to a theme park or to a cruise ship. Strap on your backpack and hit the road, the bush, or the sky. If you can't go to far off places, you can still leave the familiar, the comfortable, the fixed. New ideas and new inspiration await at every turn. Step out, Bohemian. You may not recognize yourself when you return home.

Epilogue
I Hope You'll Join Us

If you are a dreamer, come in,
If you are a dreamer, a wisher, a liar,
A hope-er, a pray-er, a magic bean buyer . . .
If you're a pretender, come sit by my fire
For we have some flax-golden tales to spin.
Come in!
Come in!

Shel Silverstein

What is a Bohemian?

I posed this question initially, with the conclusion that a Bohemian is simply someone living an unconventional life. And the very nature of "unconventionality" is difficult to define; it's a term that can't be boxed in. But after researching, studying and interviewing the people you've met in these pages, I believe certain traits and life choices show up consistently.

People living an unconventional life are risk-takers and have a high tolerance for insecurity. They are willing to step into the dark rather than stay in a safe, but uninspired cocoon. They value art, love and experience more than things and status. They don't fear money, but they aren't slaves to it either. Money is just lower on their value scale than it is for many people.

They don't watch much television, or in many cases, even have one. Creative expression is more important. They are passionate about what they do, whatever that is, and they work really, really hard at it—even if their vocation is not what pays their bills. They love the sensual, whether that be food, drink, clothes, painting, dance or sex. They have a love for,

185

respect of and connection to the natural world that exceeds the average, even if they are urbanites. They feel a kinship with nature as opposed to a desire to conquer it.

Above all, they are dreamers, schemers, and, as Shel says, magic bean buyers. They dance, sing and play the fool. They are fun people to be around. And, according to Tom Robbins, they are the true authentic seekers:

> How can one person be more real than any other? Well, some people do hide and others seek. Maybe those who are in hiding—escaping encounters, avoiding surprises, protecting their property, ignoring their fantasies, restricting their feelings, sitting out the Pan pipe, hootchy-kootch of experience—maybe those people, people who won't talk to rednecks, or if they're rednecks they won't talk to intellectuals, people who're afraid to get their shoes muddy or their noses wet, afraid to eat what they crave, afraid to drink Mexican water, afraid to bet a long shot to win, afraid to hitchhike, jaywalk, honky-tonk, cogitate, osculate, levitate, rock it, bop it, sock it, or bark at the moon, maybe such people are simply inauthentic, and maybe the jackleg humanist who says differently is due to have his tongue fried on the hot slabs of liars' hell.[ci]

As I was wrapping up this book, I signed up for an art class and set up an easel in my study for the first time in almost thirty years. Drawing 101: back to the basics. I am older than most of the students by twenty years, yet I am untroubled by that. The first day in class I became so engrossed the hours melted away like ice in spring. Later that week I stopped by my father's house to show him my first drawing and to get his feedback. After my mother had died he moved to a two-bedroom condominium and despite his negative rhetoric towards art—which never waned over the years—he set up the spare bedroom with his drawing board, equipment and supplies. The room sat ignored, but its presence alone meant something. He surprised me with his praise of my drawing, complimenting me on things that I intended as well as things he saw that I hadn't. I told him how much I was enjoying the class, but I wanted more.

"Dad, I want you to teach me what you know."

"That'll be easy—nothing. I don't remember this stuff anymore," he grumbled. I expected this response but instead of getting frustrated this time, I kept the focus on art. His art, and mine.

We continued talking and I continued asking. We went back to his studio.

"I don't have half the stuff we need, and those paints are expensive," he said. I could feel something shifting. I could afford the supplies, I told him. I wasn't quitting my day job.

"Well, I guess I can show you some technical stuff. Brush strokes and perspective and so on."

We made plans to go to the art store. A small step, but infinitely meaningful for me. And for him as well, I believe. His love for the canvas had never died. Like so many of us, he buried his passion away, misbelieving that by doing so he protected his heart from being broken by the world again.

The unconventional life is available to all of us. If enough of us give up our desperate desire for security and material escapism, our craving for the approval of others, get over our fear of failure and rejection and follow our bliss, maybe we can drop the word "unconventional" altogether, and just say that we are living. We all desperately want this. I hope you now know you are not alone, and you know you have what it takes to find and live your own unconventional life.

I hope you have expanded your idea of what it means to be Bohemian, and you will step out into the world with your soul a bit more free than it was before. And the next day a bit more, and the following day a bit more than that...continuing on and on the winding and beautiful road we share. Perhaps I'll see you at the art store, the riverside, the dance hall. I'll be watching for you.

THE BEGINNING

The Crow and the Pitcher by the author's father, Bill Downing. Photograph by the author.

Cited Works

i De Botton, Status Anxiety, New York: Pantheon Books, 2004.

ii Rigney, Francis J., and Smith, L. Douglas, The Real Bohemia,1961.

iii Kerouac, Jack, On The Road, New York: The Penguin Group, 1997.

iv Rushdie, Salman, The Ground Beneath Her Feet, New York: Henry Holt and Company, 1999.

v Kazantzakis, Nikos, Zorba the Greek, New York: Scribner, 1996.

vi Elgin, Duane, Voluntary Simplicity, New York: HarperCollins, 2010. The Stair quote was located in this source.

vii Schor, Juliet B., The Overworked American, Basic Books (1991).

viii Paquot, Thierry, The Art of the Siesta, New York: Universe Publishing, 2003.

ix Breus, Michael, "The Lark Vs. The Owl: Ingrained Sleeping Patterns," Huffington Post, December 4, 2009.

x Mednick, Sara, Take a Nap! Change Your Life, New York: Workman Publishing Company, 2006. Source initially located in The Primal Blueprint by Mark Sisson, Primal Nutrition, Inc. 2009.

xi Pink, Daniel, Drive: The Surprising Truth About What Motivates Us, New York: Riverhead Books, 2009.

xii Gladwell, Malcolm, Outliers: The Story of Success, New York: Little, Brown & Company, 2008.

xiii Powers, Ann, Weird Like Us.

xiv 2006 study conducted by Psychologist and Sexologist Serenella Salomoni.

xv Shellenbarger, Sue, "Plumbing For Joy? Be Your Own Boss," The Wall Street Journal Online, September 15, 2009.

xvi O'Farrell, John, The Best a Man Can Get, New York: Broadway Books, 2000.

xvii Fulgram, Robert, Words I Wish I Wrote, New York: Cliff Street Books, 1997. The Kent quote was located in this source.

xviii Arron, Deborah, What Can You Do With A Law Degree?, Seattle: Niche Press, 1997.

xix Allister, Betsy and Boehme, Margaret, The Writer's Almanac (July 21, 2010).

xx Jarow, Rick, The Yoga of Work, Boulder: Sounds True, Inc., 2005.

xxi Maher, John, and Briggs, Dennie, Editors, An Open Life.

xxii Lindbergh, Anne Morrow, The Gift From the Sea, New York: Pantheon Books, 2003.

xxiii Smith, Patti, Just Kids, New York: HarperCollins, 2010.

xxiv Tunney, Dr. Richard, Nottingham University's School of Psychology, 2007.

xxv Deida, David, The Way of the Superior Man, Boulder: Sounds True, Inc., 1997.

xxvi Cameron, Julia The Artist's Way, New York: Penguin Putnam, 1992.

xxvii Tosches, Nick, *In The Hands of Dante*, Boston: Little, Brown and Company, 2002.

xxviii Wolfe, Bertram, *The Incredible Life of Diego Rivera*, New York: Stein and Day, 1963.

xxix Stansky, Peter, *On Or About December 1910*, Cambridge: Harvard University Press, 1996.

xxx Gallup poll conducted November 28 through December 1, 2011 and published December 8, 2011 at Gallup.com.

xxxi Angus Deaton, Angus and Daniel Kahnemanm, Daniel, *"Does Money Buy Happiness?"* Princeton University, September 6, 2010.

xxxii Lottery winners and accident victims: is happiness relative? *Journal of Personality and Social Psychology*, 1978.

xxxiii Guillebeau, Chris, *The Art of Non-conformity*, New York: Penguin Group, 2010.

xxxiv Yates, Richard, *Revolutionary Road*, New York: Vintage Contemporaries, 2000.

xxxv Theil, Stefan, *"The Urge to Splurge,"* Newsweek, December 2010.

xxxvi Dominguez, Joe, and Robin, Vicki, *Your Money or Your Life*, New York: Penguin Books, 1999.

xxxvii Dewald, Matthew, *"Parting Words,"* University of Dayton Alumni Magazine, Summer 2011.

xxxviii Dubner, Stephen, *Freakanomics Radio*, May 16, 2012.

xxxix McCullough, David, G., et al., *The Wyeths; A Father And His Family*, Washington, D.C., Greater Washington Educational Telecommunications Association, Inc., 1986.

191

xl A Single Man, Columbia TriStar Home Entertainment, 2010.

xli Gilbert, Elizabeth, Eat, Pray, Love, New York: Penguin, 2006.

xlii Kundera, Milan, Slowness, New York: HarperPerennial, 1997.

xliii Jones, Malcom, "Slow Nation," Newsweek, July 12, 2010.

xliv Begley, Louis, About Schmidt, New York, Ballantine Books, 1997.

xlv Rosenfield, Alvin, M.D, and Wise, Nicole, The Over-Scheduled Child: Avoiding the Hyper-Parenting Trap, New York: St. Martin's Press, 2000.

xlvi Honore, Carl, In Praise of Slowness, New York: HarperCollins, 2004.

xlvii Powell, Richard, Wabi Sabi Simple, Avon: CWL Publishing Enterprises, Inc., 2005.

xlviii Sternberg, Dr. Esther M., Healing Spaces, Cambridge: Harvard University Press, 2009.

xlix Study published in the Journal of Alternative and Complementary Medicine and reported in Spirituality and Health, March/April 2011.

l"Don't let chaos get you down," Newsweek, Nov. 7 & 14 2011.

li Ueland, Brenda, If You Want to Write, Saint Paul: Graywolf Press, 1938.

lii Flocker, Michael, The Hedonism Handbook, Cambridge: Da Capo Press, 2004.

liii Maher, John, and Briggs, Dennie, Editors, An Open Life, New York: Harper & Row, 1989.

liv Tzu, Lao, Tao Te Ching, Mitchell, Stephen, translator, New York: Harper Peren-

nial,1988. All quotations included from Tao Te Ching are from the Stephen Mitchell translation.

lv Francis, John, Planet Walker, Washington, D.C.: National Geographic Books, 2008.

lvi Yutang, Lin, The Importance of Living.

lvii Hendricks, Gay, A Year of Living Consciously, New York: HarperCollins, 1998.

lviii Sweeney, Richard J., Coming of Age: A Jungian View of Maturity, 2012.

lix Hodgkinson, Tom, How to Be Idle, New York: Harper Perennial, 2006.

lx Key, Wilson Bryan, Subliminal Seduction, Englewood Cliffs: Prentice Hall, Inc., 1973.

lxi Dass, Ram, Journey of Awakening, New York: Bantam Books, 1990.

lxii Barret, Deirdre, Supernormal Stimuli, New York: W.W. Norton & Company, 2010.

lxiii Franzen, Jonathan, How To Be Alone, New York: Picador, 2002.

lxiv Tolle, Eckhart, The Power of Now, Novato: New World Library, 1999.

lxv quote located in Robert Fulgram's Words I Wish I Wrote.

lxvi Robinson, Ken, "Schools Kill Creativity," TED Talks, 2006.

lxvii Gardner, Howard, The Arts and Human Development, New York: Wiley, 1973.

lxviii Carey, John, What Good Are The Arts?, New York: Oxford University Press, 2006.

lxix Cohen, Gene D., M.D., Ph.D., The Creative Age: Awakening Human Potential in the Second Half of Life, New York: Quill, 2001.

lxx The Writer's Almanac, 3/22/10.

lxxi The Writer's Almanac, 11/19/09.

lxxii The Writer's Almanac, 11/20/09.

lxxiii Gladwell, Malcolm, Outliers.

lxxiv Gladwell, Malcolm, "Late Bloomers," The New Yorker, October 2008.

lxxv Wayne, Kenneth, "Matisse: the Genius as Late Bloomer," The New Criterion January 1999.

lxxvi Richards, Keith, Life, Little, Brown and Company, 2010.

lxxvii McCullough, David, G., et al., The Wyeths; A Father And His Family.

lxxviii Bronson, Po, and Merryman, Ashley, "Creativity in America," Newsweek, July 19, 2010.

lxxix Chopra, Deepak, Magical Mind, Magical Body, Simon & Schuster, New York, 2003.

lxxx Norris, Kathleen, Acedia, New York: Riverhead, 2008.

lxxxi Keyes, Ralph, The Courage to Write, New York: Henry Holt & Company, 1995.

lxxxii The Writers Almanac, 2/17/11.

lxxxiii Tosches, In The Hands of Dante.

lxxxiv Grossman, Lev, "Books Gone Wild: The Digital Age Reshapes Literature," Time,

The Abundant Bohemian

January 21, 2009.

lxxxv Hillman, James, The Soul's Code, Random House, 1996.

lxxxvi Jasiewicz, Isia, "Who Needs a Publisher?" Newsweek, August 2010.

lxxxvii Katz, Jamie, "Find Your Inner Genius," AARP Magazine, December 2008.

lxxxviii The Census Bureau's 2006 Statistical Abstract of the United States.

lxxxix Gilbert, Elizabeth, Eat, Pray, Love.

xc McDougall, Christopher, Born to Run, New York: Vintage Books, 2009.

xci Stansky, Peter, On or About December 1910.

xcii Stanksy, Peter, On or About December 1910.

xciii Perel, Ester, from an interview with The Idler, "Carnal Knowledge," #40, 2007.

xciv Robbins, Tom, Still Life With Woodpecker.

xcv Robbins, Tom, Still Life With Woodpecker.

xcvi Verghese, Joe, et. al., "Leisure Activities and the Risk of Dementia in the Elderly," New England Journal of Medicine, June 19, 2003.

xcvii Auster, Paul, Winter Journal, Newy York: Henry Holt and Company, 2012.

xcviii Sideways, Beverly Hills, 20th Century Fox Home Entertainment, 2005.

xcix Bleeker, Dr. Margrit L., and Ford, Patrick D., "Impact of Cognitive Reserve on the Relationship of Lead Exposure and Neurobehavioral Performance," Neurology, the

Joseph Downing

Journal of the American Academy of Neurology, April 1, 2008.

c Heat-Moon, William, Blue Highway, New York: Back Bay Books, 1999.

ci Robbins, Tom, Still Life With Woodpecker, New York: Bantam Books, 1980.

196

About the Author
Joseph Downing

Joe is a writer and attorney residing in Dayton, Ohio. You can read his blog at www.abundantbohemian.com and can contact him at joe@abundantbohemian.com to share your own Bohemian success stories.

Made in the USA
Monee, IL
16 March 2021